Ubiquitous Relativity:
My Truth is Not the Truth

Ian Winer

11664 National Blvd, #345
Los Angeles, CA. 90064
310-584-1504
www.TVGuestpert Publishing.com
www.TVGuestpert.com

First Printing June 2019
10 9 8 7 6 5 4 3 2 1

UBIQUITOUS RELATIVITY

MY **TRUTH** IS NOT **THE TRUTH**

Ian Winer

INVESTOR • PHILOSOPHER • HUMANITARIAN

Acknowledgments

The people in my life have made it possible for me to take this journey. With a seemingly infinite amount of patience, my wife Kelly has helped me through the highs and lows of writing a book. I want to thank my editor Dana Breseman for her professionalism and patience and Richard Janes, who has helped develop my personal brand. I'd also like to thank Alexandria Rogers for helping to get this book over the finish line. And to Dr. Louise Banks; thanks for the inspiration.

To Kelly

Table of Contents

"Judge not, that ye be not judged

"For with what judgment ye judge, ye shall be judged: and with what measure ye mete, it shall be measured to you again.

"And why beholdest thou the mote that is in thy brother's eye, but considerest not the beam that is in thine own eye?"

Matthew 7:1-3

Why *Ubiquitous Relativity* Is Vital to Our Lives

I Am No Angel.

For the last twenty-two years, I have worked as a stock trader, but I always dreamt I would be a fiction writer someday. Instead, I am espousing philosophy. Like everyone, I am a basket of contradictions.

I have given to charities, been a loving husband and a loyal friend. I have sought wealth by all means, failed in marriage, and avoided connections with others. I have had millions in cash and I have had creditors looking for me after I accrued hundreds of thousands of dollars in debt. I drove a BMW 750 at age twenty-nine, only to have it re-possessed. I have lived in a beautiful house, only to sell it short a few years later. I have been in the depths of addiction and have successfully returned to sobriety. I have served as a role model in management by being fair, honorable, and taking care of my people. I have made numerous leadership errors because I was inflexible, over-confident, and motivated people by scaring them.

I have spent my entire life with the highest conviction in my beliefs. I assumed that I possessed the ability to perfectly judge any situation and anybody's motivations. I could describe the facts of any encounter and everyone involved as confidently as if I were proclaiming the sky was blue. For me, this was simply human nature. I was often wrong, but never in doubt.

While I was a cadet at West Point, one of my sergeants once told me: "If you keep your eyes and ears open and your mouth shut, then you might just learn something." I never listened.

Until recently, I accepted as fact that we humans share one world within one universe. Concepts like world peace, songs like "This Land Is Your Land," and events like Earth Day appealed to me because they represent lofty goals of working together to achieve a Utopia.[1] However, although these aims of sharing one universe in harmony sound wonderful, I always found my emotions and personal judgments kept this goal out of my reach. Perhaps I needed to open myself to the possibility that my personal world is not the only world.

Almost two-thirds of Americans report being stressed about the future of the nation, according to a recent *Stress in America* survey from the American Psychological Association.[2] But do we have to live our lives stressed about our future? What can we do to unburden ourselves of this fear?

Ubiquitous Relativity is about challenging our long-held beliefs about the world and everyone in it. This book asks each of us to take a leap of faith into the unknown, the uncomfortable, and the unfamiliar. *Ubiquitous Relativity* makes one basic assumption: our lives are incomplete without human connection. If you agree with this assumption and want to forge stronger connections, then the philosophy outlined in this book could offer a route towards a more fulfilling life.

Since the beginning of human history, millions of people have devised methods to make it easier to connect with others. *Ubiquitous Relativity* does not mandate anything. It isn't concerned with laws or pillars that must be followed without deviation. This philosophy is about asking people to question their assumptions about the world around them.

Many of us reach a point in life where we wonder, "Can I really make a difference during my time on Earth?" I have asked myself this question too many times to remember – and I have concluded that the answer is a definitive "Yes."

This book takes a unique approach to "making a difference." I propose a way to positively impact the world using a simple concept. There are many ways to change the lives of others, from donating to charities to researching medical advancements to acting as a role model to children. *Ubiquitous Relativity* considers a less conventional way to make a difference. This book challenges readers to question their beliefs and test their judgments. Asking ourselves "What do we not know?" as opposed to "What do we know?" creates an opportunity to change the world for the better. Hopefully, at the end of this book, we will be able to turn inward to turn outward. We may be able to disconnect from our biases to connect with others. We may be able to understand how people do and say things that seem unconscionable to us. The world can become less frightening and more hopeful. It has for me.

This book aims to help readers appreciate the possibility that *my* world is not *the* world. As a victim of abuse, I have struggled with accepting this reality. I always believed that the facts of my life, as I saw them, were the way everyone should see them. When I recall my own suffering, I remember every detail. I always expected the people who hurt me to also remember every detail the same way I did. Accepting that there will always be a stark difference between *my* truth and *the* truth has helped me bridge that gap and heal. If you struggle with this as well, this book may help.

Many of us know the famous poem "The Road Not Taken" by Robert Frost and remember the lines:

> *Two roads diverged in a wood, and I— I took the one less traveled by, and that has made all the difference.*[3]

The "two roads" analogy implies that the roads and the choice between them can look very similar for everyone. Like most artistic expression, the actual meaning of Frost's work is debatable – but common interpretation views it as a call to make choices that are less popular but are ultimately more rewarding. The choices we make shape our world. I realized that this is the life metaphor I have been using for forty-four years, but it hasn't helped me to understand the world. I often chose to go in the wrong direction.

Recently, I questioned the application of this "two roads" analogy. I began to wonder if there are actually an infinite number of parallel roads, and each person is traveling their own route, along their own road.

Each person moves at a different speed, and no two lanes are the same. The passages resemble each other only in their linearity. If I am on my path, I may look left or right and see others traveling, but I cannot see what obstacles they have overcome in their road, nor can I see what they have learned throughout their journeys.

Over the course of my life, my biggest challenge has been judging the other paths and the people who travel on them. Making these judgments each day often prevented me from connecting with other people.

How can I remodel my life and the way that I approach other people? What if I paused for a second to think about someone else's avenue in life before I judged them? Why is it so darn hard to accept that I simply do not know the truth about the people and paths around me? Why do I believe we are all given directions at the beginning of our lives to succeed, as long as we choose to follow an approved societal course? Why do I look at my parallel travelers and insist that they need to look at my directions in order to reach the goal at the end of their roads? How do I stop trying to apply universal principles to a relative world?

This epiphany came when I least expected it, and it happened in a very embarrassing fashion. I had just had nasal surgery to repair a deviated septum. I was sitting in my car at a stoplight, with my finger up my nose to help with the pain. In the car next to me, a woman stopped and looked at me in disgust. In her universe, through her eyes, this woman saw a man picking his nose at a stoplight. I cannot tell you what she thought, but I can say definitively that she did not know that I was recovering from nasal surgery.

Shortly after that moment at the intersection, I visited the Musée de l'Orangerie in Paris and had the privilege of seeing Claude Monet's "Water Lilies". This work of art is a mural of eight enormous landscapes of foliage in still water.[4] As I gazed at the paintings, I began to notice colors I had not seen just a moment before. I looked around at the one hundred or so people in the room, and each of us was looking at different parts of the collection. I thought how incredible it was that we were each having our own experience and seeing new colors at every moment, in completely different orders. Just as importantly, each person must also have a personal emotional trigger at the sight of those paintings. What did each person sense? What did each person feel? We were all physically in the same area of the same museum, yet we occupied distinct universes.

We see the world and make judgments and come to conclusions, all based only on the information in our universe.

Is the homeless man on the street a failure, as I might imagine, or did his parents abandon him at a young age, leaving him without material goods or savings? What if his universe is totally different from mine? Who am I to judge him?

If I accept the basic premise that each universe operates in its own manner, then I can begin to let go of my desire to judge everything. Instead, I can strive to reach a place of acceptance.

When Albert Einstein developed his theory of relativity, he changed the world forever. Isaac Newton's laws were no longer believed to be universal – instead, measuring the speed of objects in motion depended on where you were within the universe. So if I am walking on a train, my measure of my speed is different than the people who are watching the train travel by them. Brian Greene, in his book *The Fabric of the Cosmos*, comments on Einstein's theory of Special Relativity as it relates to time:

> *Observers moving relative to each other have a different conception of what exists at a given moment, and hence they have different concep-tions of reality.*[5]

If that law could apply to objects in motion, I wondered if it could also apply to the entire human experience.

This is **Ubiquitous Relativity**: the notion that each individual uniquely senses the universe and that each individual's reaction to those senses is a direct result of unique experiences over the course of a lifetime. For these reasons, no two people's universes are the same and we know virtually nothing about any universe except our own.

From the *Merriam-Webster Dictionary:*
> **Ubiquitous** comes to us from the noun "ubiquity," meaning "pres-ence everywhere or in many places simultaneously." Ubiquitous is derived from the Latin word for "everywhere," which is *ubique.*[6]

Relativity is the state of being dependent for existence on or determined in nature, value, or quality by relation to something else.[7]

In a mathematical formula, a world of Ubiquitous Relativity can be expressed as an infinite number of senses multiplied by an infinite number of emotions triggered by those senses.

This is what I call the Everlasting Equation:

So what is the result of multiplying these two infinities? A mathematician may say that the problem here is that you are regarding infinity as a number. You cannot multiply infinity by infinity, for it cannot be represented as an integer. It represents a symbol for a value that is so large that we can't imagine it. Indeed, emotions and senses are not integers or numbers. They have no quantifiable boundary. So, when we judge others, if we try to imagine the boundless possibilities of their senses and emotions, we may find:

We each live in our own universe.

A visual representation of *Ubiquitous Relativity* looks like double-paned windows. The first piece of glass represents the physiological act of sensing something. Each person has a unique width of glass to his or her specific body, just as people literally sense things differently given their genetic and physiological traits. The second piece of glass is also unique to each person and represents the emotion triggered by a person's history of inputs associated with that sense. Light comes into contact with a window, just as sensations of all kinds affect people. The light contorts as it penetrates both panes of the glass. The same happens with people. The world we sense changes as it comes into our unique universe.

Ubiquitous Relativity is designed to tweak people's judgments ever so slightly, so that we may all have a little more understanding and a little more patience. Without communication and human contact, life is extraordinarily difficult. I have romanticized the lone wolf existence, only to find that the reality was I missed the connection to others. I have found that true human contact and relationships require me to question my biases. If I accept that I live in a world of *Ubiquitous Relativity*, then the only logical way to interact is to pause on my judgments. It is this pause in judgment that can make the difference between the roads we travel.

This book is divided into five parts. In Part One, I'll discuss how a difficult childhood laid the groundwork for the philosophy of *Ubiquitous Relativity*. It is critical to understand why humans crave certainty and how we tend to search for universality. By definition, *Ubiquitous Relativity* asks us to move away from generalizations, so we need to begin this analysis by understanding why we seek sureness and the forms this quest has taken over our history. In modern times, the rapid ascent of technology has necessitated new approaches to human connections.

In Part Two, we'll examine the left side of the Everlasting Equation by examining how unique we are in terms of our physical abilities. We will try to answer the question, "How do the physiological differences between us alter how we sense the world?"

In Part Three, we'll study the right side of our Everlasting Equation and the infinite number of emotions triggered by these sensations. We will look at multiple examples of everyday situations in detail, and consider how appreciating a world of *Ubiquitous Relativity* can change the perceptions of everyone involved.

In Part Four, we will look at how Finance and Investing influence a world of *Ubiquitous Relativity*. I explore how everything I have learned in the stock market and business world integrate with this new philosophy.

Finally, in Part Five, I'll share some exercises and practices I use to help me pause in judgment and to appreciate my unique universe. Of course, these methods may not work for everyone, as I can only speak to my own experience. My way is the right way for me and me alone.

If I can look at another person and approach them as a formula with no universal solution, then perhaps I can acknowledge I know very little about the infinite combinations of senses and emotions that make them just as human as I am.

The population of the world is roughly 7.5 billion.[8] It is hard to imagine a number that large, let alone to consider that number in terms of human lives. Can one expect any universal thoughts or qualities among so many people? The interesting paradox is that I would answer that question with a definitive "No," yet I expect universal qualities in even the most basic of the hundreds of interactions I experience each day. When I greet others, I expect that they say hello to me my way and at my time.

Restraining my impulses and questioning my judgment is a daily battle. With each new person I meet, I must remember that we each look at everything around us through different lenses.

Each time we meet another person we have the opportunity to see things differently, even if only for a moment. I aim for progress and progress alone in changing my perceptions. But imagine if each of the 7.5 billion people on the planet were to pause on a judgment for one moment a day. Perhaps we could change the world.

PART 1:

Why Is Now the Time for Ubiquitous Relativity?

CHAPTER 1

MY TRUTH

"Beauty is truth, truth beauty, – that is all Ye know on earth, and all ye need to know." [9]

– John Keats

From the moment at the stoplight to the experience at the Musée d l'Orangerie, there were specific moments when I started to appreciate a world of *Ubiquitous Relativity*. I wondered why, after forty-three years, I was suddenly experiencing situations that opened my mind to this new way of thinking. It felt like I had been walking in darkness and someone had handed me night vision goggles. What had changed? I was not on a vision quest, nor even actively trying to develop my spirituality. So why was this clarity occurring now?

Countless philosophers have spent lifetimes analyzing the interplay of conscious and unconscious thoughts that makes us human. As Carl Jung said, "Until you make the unconscious conscious, it will direct your life and you will call it fate." [10] I wondered, did I experience these events consciously and change my thinking as a result? Or had I already been thinking of this philosophy subconsciously, and these events simply brought this way of thinking to my newly awakened mind? In a way, this question is a psychological example of the classic dilemma of whether the chicken or the egg came first. As I struggled with these questions, I began to piece together the idea of *Ubiquitous Relativity*. It was simultaneously enlightening and horrifying to realize that the seeds of this concept had been planted in my mind since my earliest memories. It only took a little over four decades for those seeds to start growing above the surface.

Like too many other young children, I was the victim of constant physical and verbal abuse from a very young age. This lasted until I left my parents' house at sixteen years old. For most of my life, I believed not only that I deserved the abuse from my parents, but also that any major successes I have ever had were because of the abuse. "It made me tough," I told myself. "This is why I can handle adversity." I held these beliefs without question, and I wore them on my chest as a combat soldier wears medals. I was proud of my upbringing because nothing ever seemed to rattle me – which kept me safe in what I viewed as an inherently dangerous world. I was so afraid to remember the abuse that I had drawn a causal relationship between the beatings and the moments in my life where I felt the most pride. Defense mechanisms come in many shapes and forms, and my defense was to blame myself for the abuse and justify it as fair punishment. Like many coping methods, it worked until it didn't.

Everyone reacts differently to the terrors of growing up in a terrible household. As I grew older and moved further away from the actual abuse, I coped by laughing about the torment with my two younger brothers. We would shake our heads and tell stories. The fake laughter helped us avoid the reality of our past.

Although I knew the crimes were real, I still searched for ways to excuse the criminals. I considered pardoning my parents' behavior, just like a court might judge someone too insane to stand trial. I thought, clearly they are mentally ill, because no sane person would have treated their children this way. Unlike today, therapy and medication were in short supply back when they were parenting, so they didn't have the tools necessary for success. I believed if I told myself this enough, I would be able to reach a place of acceptance. I was wrong.

Did my parents ever show remorse? My father could only drum up the occasional, "I know I wasn't a perfect father." My mother, every once in a very long while, would say, "I should have done more to protect you." I accepted those half-hearted apologies and even felt some sympathy when my dad would say: "You think you had it tough? You should have seen how my father treated me."

Imagine that. I felt sympathy for a man who had a clear choice to stop or continue the cycle of violence he had experienced as a child – and who chose to pass on the abuse.

Time moved on as it does – slow days and quick years. My brothers and I grew up and built families of our own. My mother and father divorced when I was twenty, and both moved on to new relationships. Occasionally, weddings or birthdays would bring us all together, but nobody ever really acknowledged the past. That was perfectly fine with me. By my mid-twenties, I had turned to alcohol and drugs to self-medicate any pain I still carried with me from my childhood. I walked through life in a fog that never moved out to sea.

A little over five years ago, that murkiness finally began to clear. I began my journey into a sober life. Soon after, I began intensive therapy around much of the wreckage that I carried with me as a result of growing up in that wretched environment. I began to understand why I was uncomfortable all the time and why I was so defensive – I yearned for total control of everything and everyone around me, because as a child that had been the only way I could avoid a beating. I still got chills if anyone even touched me on the back of my neck or shoulders. I carried the burden of abuse in everything. I spent my entire existence living in fear.

A combination of a clear mind and a lot of pain without any anesthetic shook me awake. Suddenly, there was an inflection point in my analysis of my abuse. I was with my therapist and discussing the weight of the abuse I carried with me each day. He asked me, "Why do you excuse your parents from this burden? Why must you be alone in justifying it? Isn't it time you believed the reality of the abuse?" I finally realized that the brutality I experienced as a young child was not funny. My parents' actions could not simply be excused as insanity. Their tepid remorse – essentially paying lip service to their theft of my youth – was no longer enough for me.

About six months into writing this book, I concluded that the only way for me to begin to recover was to confront my mother and father. My parents needed to know the truth. They had to understand that I remembered every detail of the abuse, and that – no matter how much they skirt around the past – I would not allow them to keep living in blissful ignorance. I rehearsed that conversation many times and I imagined my parents in tears, regretting all the wrong they had ever done to me. I fantasized about them apologizing to me and then atoning for their sins. My parents would know the truth – but unlike in the Bible, it would set me free.[11]

As I prepared to visit each of them for what I thought would surely be a climactic and cathartic experience, I awoke one night with an awful thought: what if telling my parents *the* truth was really only telling them *my* truth? Could it be possible that their memories were actually very different than mine? I tried to reassure myself that they would certainly acknowledge the facts as I knew them – but no matter how many hours I spent trying to convince myself, I was no longer even remotely confident in that belief. In fact, the only conclusions I could make about their memories were that a) I did not know what they were, and b) It was next-to-impossible that they would be the same as mine. My hopes for a moment of lucidity with each of my parents faded away.

It was around this time that the woman saw me at the stoplight with my finger up my nose. As she looked at me with disgust, I understood that she did not know what was going on in my universe. Put differently, she did not know my truth. Likewise, I did not know what she was experiencing at that moment. I did not know her truth. It all started to make sense to me – except I still could not figure out how my parents fit into this. Wouldn't it be inconsistent to say that each person lives in his or her own universe – but to have a different standard for my parents? Could I logically claim that each person has their own truth – except for my parents, who need to have my truth when we remember the abuse? If I answer these questions honestly, then I have to admit that my plans for this meeting with my mom and dad were at odds with my own philosophy.

I struggle with this to this very moment. I believe absolutely in this philosophy of *Ubiquitous Relativity*, yet I want my parents to agree to my version of every event in my childhood. I know in my heart that – as much as it pains me to admit – their truths will be different than my truth.

I have not confronted my parents. I chose instead to write this book and see where it takes me. I may talk to them someday and share my truth, with no expectation for anything in return. But that would require accepting that someone who did a terrible thing to me may have a different version of those same events, and that there is nothing I can do to make my truth become their truths. And this is one of the most difficult things in life.

I live in a world of *Ubiquitous Relativity*, where each person lives in their own universe. Each person senses the world differently and reacts to those senses differently. We know very little about even our closest friends' universe and they know almost nothing about ours. But with questions like "Why do you think that way?" and "How do you remember things?" we can start to connect on a different level – and, if we are very lucky, we can start to pause on judgment.

CHAPTER 2

THE ILLUSION OF UNIVERSALITY

*"Dream delivers us to dream, and there is no end to illusion. Life is like a train of moods like a string of beads, and, as we pass through them, they prove to be many-colored lenses which paint the world their own hue..."*12

–Ralph Waldo Emerson

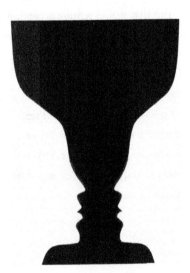

Take a close look at the image above; most of us have seen this image at one point or another. What do you see? Can you see two different images in this double optical illusion? Do you see the white silhouettes of two people facing each other or do you see a black drinking cup? The nature of my question implies a certain binary outcome: either you see the cup, or you see the silhouettes.

What if I asked you what you see but didn't give two choices? You may say you see a goblet, a cup, a chalice, or a wine glass. Alternatively, you may see the faces of two people, two colorless faces leaning in to kiss each other, two faces of the same sex, or identical twins. You may see multiple images or none at all. Your eyes process the image for your brain to interpret, and what you see is determined by your unique physiological programming. But what do these different visions actually mean for your judgment of the picture? How does the image that you see make you feel?

Understanding the answer to those questions is paramount to appreciating a world of *Ubiquitous Relativity*. Upon seeing the image, there are infinite possible emotions you could feel. Could two people see a goblet but react differently to this goblet? If, for example, my friend Mark sees a goblet, it may make him picture a Thanksgiving dinner with his family, full of joy and warmth. The image triggers the memory based on his experiences with goblets over the course of his lifetime. If this is a happy memory for him, he may feel better after looking at the image. I could look at the same image and see a goblet as well. I may associate that image with a Thanksgiving dinner with my family, filled with anguish and stress. Again, the image triggers a memory based on my own life experience. If these memories are painful, I may feel worse after looking at the image. Mark and I can look at the exact same image and identify it as the same image – yet we can have completely different feelings due to the memories in each of our universes.

What would you feel after seeing a goblet or hearing the word "goblet"? What memories are triggered based on the experiences in your universe? We can even take this a step further by examining the reactions each of us has if we see different images in the optical illusion pictured in the beginning of this chapter. If I look at the black center of the optical illusion, I may see it as a goblet – or I may see it as a chalice, a cup, a trophy, an urn, and so on. Each of those words may engender distinct memories for me, and, as a function of those memories, completely different emotions.

It is easy to see how the specific words we use to define an image can take us in dramatically different emotional directions. Imagine two people: one who recently won a big championship, and one who just lost a title. They may each see a trophy, but it would evoke different memories based on their own unique experiences.

We can also combine these scenarios. Imagine one person sees a goblet, and another sees a trophy. Even as they look at the same image, they perceive it differently and may have distinct emotional reactions.

People could see infinite combinations of images and feel infinite combinations of emotions. The crux of *Ubiquitous Relativity* rests on this dynamic – because of this dynamic, we know very little about what someone else is sensing or feeling.

Using the example of the goblet, consider that after my friend Mark and I see that image, I may start to feel distressed because of the experiences in my universe. Mark, on the other hand, may feel better. He may struggle to understand how that image could upset me. If he can tell that I am upset, he may judge my reaction based solely on the information in his universe. He may say, "What's got you down? Doesn't that goblet just make you want to sit at a big dinner table and eat a huge meal with the family?"

If I simply respond "No," he may judge my attitude with little to no knowledge of my experience. He may conclude I am not particularly warm, or that I'm too introverted. If my friend doesn't ask why I feel the way I do, he will never begin to understand why a goblet in my universe is different than a goblet in his universe.

Each of us uniquely senses the world and each of us has unique emotional reactions to those senses. If I judge someone else's senses and emotions based on the experiences in my universe, that is when conflict is likely to ensue. The goblet-silhouette optical illusion is just one example of the infinite possibilities of senses and emotions. Imagine all the stimuli that could cause us to remember Thanksgiving dinner and thereby trigger the same conflict. We could each smell the same turkey, touch the same tablecloth, hear the same holiday music, or taste the same cranberries – and wind up in polar opposite moods.

In future chapters, we will take a much more in-depth look at the way physical senses take us to different emotional places, and we will explore the conflicts that arise when we apply the laws of our universe to someone else's universe.

This is the twofold illusion of universality. The first illusion is that people sense the world in exactly the same way. The second illusion is that people react emotionally to those senses in precisely the same fashion. Despite this, we still crave certainty in our senses and emotions. We will try to explain this desire in the next chapter.

CHAPTER 3

OUR CRAVING FOR CERTAINTY

"If a man will begin with certainties, he shall end in doubts; but if he will be content to begin with doubts, he shall end in certainties." [13]

– Francis Bacon

Imagine that as part of an exercise in "mandatory fun" at the company you work for, your department has organized a ten-kilometer running race against one of the other departments. The CEO has authorized the winning team to take a day off from work after the race. The competition is in about a month, and it is time to get into running shape. You go online and decide to call the first two running clubs you see in your search. The first club describes its method:

Our classes are every Monday, Wednesday, and Friday at 8:00 a.m. As a member of this class, you will run five miles in forty minutes each session.

The second running club also details its training technique:

Our class times will change each week and we will call you the night before to let you know when we are running. At each session, you will be told to start running and at some point you will be told when to stop.

Which running regimen would you choose? In the first running club, there is certainty, and in the second, uncertainty. Most people would prefer the first mode of training because they know when they are running, how far they have to go, and at what speed they will need to run. The second program may offer better training, but there is no guarantee or even any certainty about the details of the program, as the people in the class have no idea when they will be running, what speed they are supposed to run, or any idea what distance they will ultimately travel.

The fear of the unknown, whether in matters as small as an unopened credit

9

card bill or as large as what happens when we die, is a driving force behind many of the choices humans make. This instinct to avoid uncertainty keeps us safe. At the same time, this apprehension deprives us of many human connections; we tend to surround ourselves with what we find familiar and certain. The fear of what we do not know fuels our desire to identify universal laws of nature – laws that stretch across all aspects of our lives and belief systems.

Physicists and mathematicians have formulated universal equations to make sense of our physical world. These equations are considered proofs of truth. Anyone who has struggled through algebra (like me) knows that one of the most common mathematical formulas is the Pythagorean Theorem,[14] which describes the relationship between the sides of a right triangle. A right triangle consists of two legs and a hypotenuse. The two legs meet at a ninety-degree angle. The hypotenuse, the side opposite the right angle, is the longest side of the right triangle.

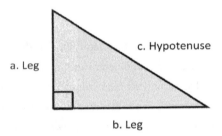

The Pythagorean Theorem tells us that in every right triangle, the square of the length of the hypotenuse (c in the above image) is equal to the sum of the squared lengths of the other two lengths (a and b). In other words,

$a2 + b2 = c2.$[15]

Based on the mathematical laws of our universe, we have determined that the Pythagorean Theorem is always true, and it has been accepted as fact since the sixth century.

We accept many mathematical relationships as universal fact, including the simple equation below:

$2 + 2 = 4$

Almost anybody who has learned basic math would unquestioningly accept this as true in every situation. However, things get interesting when we try to apply the same standards of absolute certainty to areas outside mathematics.

Many people and cultures view their moral codes as universal, in the same vein as they believe that 2 + 2 = 4. This is the source of many conflicts and it is one of the main obstacles to human connection. There are laws of nature that all people seem to agree upon, and then there are laws of human behavior that we seemingly cannot agree upon at all. Belief systems based on these so-called laws of human behavior have led to a never-ending cycle of conflict, because people view their personal perspectives as if they were mathematical laws of nature. Why is this?

One of the greatest unknowns is what happens to us when we die. For millennia, religions of the world have created commandments. We can think of these as attempts to establish universal moral codes that, if followed, promise to lead to either a wonderful afterlife, some form of reward when we pass away, or the ability to claim to live a good life at the present moment. For instance, in the Old Testament, the way to live was given directly to the Jewish people from God:

The Ten Commandments:[16]

1 You shall have no other gods before Me.

2 You shall make no idols.

3 You shall not take the name of the Lord your God in vain.

4 Keep the Sabbath day holy.

5 Honor your father and your mother.

6 You shall not murder.

7 You shall not commit adultery.

8 You shall not steal.

9 You shall not bear false witness against your neighbor.

10 You shall not covet.

This universal approach to a "right" way of living exists in other religions outside of the Judeo-Christian belief system as well:

The Five Pillars of Islam are the Foundation of Muslim life:[17]

1 Faith or belief in the Oneness of God and the finality of the prophethood of Muhammad.

2 Establishment of the daily prayers.

3 Concern for and almsgiving to the needy.

4 Self-purification through fasting.

5 The pilgrimage to Makkah for those who are able.

Less traditional belief systems can also serve as guides to enlightenment. When I search "universal law" on Google, the first few results all point to a book published in 1988: The Light Shall Set You Free by Dr. Norma J. Milanovich and Dr. Shirley McCune. In the book, the authors state there are twelve universal laws and twenty-one sub-laws that describe ways in which cause and effect are related. These universal laws can also be viewed as guidelines for behaviors that will enhance our physical, mental, emotional, and spiritual growth.[18]

Universal Laws:

1. The Law of Divine Oneness

2. The Law of Vibration

3. The Law of Action

4. The Law of Correspondence

5. The Law of Cause and Effect

6. The Law of Compensation

7. The Law of Attraction

8. The Law of Perpetual Transmutation of Energy

9. The Law of Relativity

10. The Law of Polarity

11. The Law of Rhythm

12. The Law of Gender

The term "universal law" implies that this law is followed by all people or things in the world, that it's a statement of fact deduced from observation, and that it always occurs if certain conditions are present.[19][20]

"Enlightenment" means different things to different people, but society generally views this concept as a higher state of consciousness and an admirable goal to pursue. So if a spiritual advisor gives us universal laws to attain spiritual growth, the advisor is creating certainty. In Buddhism, enlightenment is that awareness which frees a person from the cycle of rebirth.[21] The certainty in The Light Shall Set You Free is that people will achieve spiritual growth if they follow the twelve universal laws. In this context, "universal" means spiritual growth is possible for anyone and "law" implies that the tenets should be rigidly followed without exception.

There are also other credos that we as a society frame as universal.

The Golden Rule:

"Therefore all things whatsoever ye would do that men should do to you; do ye even so to them."[22]

The Golden Rule seems logical enough to be called "golden" and a "rule" – except for one major flaw. The assumption in this maxim is that others would like to be treated the same way we would like to be treated. The problem with this rule is that what may be pure joy for me could be a source of incredible pain for someone else. For instance, I like to chat with strangers. If I see someone sitting on a bus alone, I will sit down next to them and try to start a conversation, because I would like the same to happen if I were sitting alone somewhere. By following the Golden Rule, I am simply doing to others as I would like to be done to me. But what if that stranger does not want to talk right now? What if the stranger is a misanthrope or has work to do and needs to concentrate? What if the stranger is engrossed in a book? There are many other examples of how the Golden Rule loses some of its shine. The bottom line is that if an edict is to be considered a rule, then it should have universal application – and it is unclear if the Golden Rule fits that description.

I am not the first person to question the Golden Rule in this fashion. Tony Alessandra, in his book *The Platinum Rule*, posits a new way of looking at things: "Treat others the way they want to be treated."[23] This rule seems like an improvement – except how do we really know how others want to be treated? We could ask each person, "How would you like to be treated?" But each situation is different, and people change throughout their lives. So the way a person may want to be treated is not static, but in fact very dynamic. It could be as simple as the way a person wants to be treated before or after their first cup of coffee in the morning! In a world of *Ubiquitous Relativity*, the search for certainty needs to be deemphasized. Therefore, caution is necessary when applying rules to life.

I have tried to live by many of the laws discussed above. I have sought rules and then tried my best to follow them. All my life, I yearned to be told what to do rather than have to puzzle out my own best way to live. As I explore a new way of thinking in a world of *Ubiquitous Relativity*, I am trying to fight my desire for universal answers. This has been very difficult for me, because it requires that I move significantly outside of my comfort zone.

Remember the definition of *Ubiquitous Relativity*: the notion that each individual person uniquely senses the universe and that each individual's reactions to those senses are a direct result of unique experiences over the course of a lifetime. For these reasons, no two people's universes are the same and we know virtually nothing about any universe except our own.

This logically engenders the following argument: "If we truly believe in a world of *Ubiquitous Relativity*, then how do we have any laws in society? Can't people just say, 'I committed murder, but in my universe, this is acceptable?'"

Recall that our philosophy does not say there are no universal laws. Clearly, committing a murder is unacceptable within our society. But in a world of *Ubiquitous Relativity*, it is important to ask, "What had to happen in these murderers' lives to get them to this point? How did this criminal's best thinking result in this heinous act?" By asking these questions, we may begin to realize some small part of the genesis of this terrible act.

Remember, we are not justifying behavior nor asking for the victim to forgive the perpetrator. In a world of *Ubiquitous Relativity*, we simply believe there is value in questioning what we do not know about the people perpetrating these acts. "Did they ever have a chance themselves? How was their childhood?"

We often witness these terrible acts on the news or read about them – and in some cases, we experience them ourselves. The reality is nearly impossible to believe. We are left wondering the why and the how of it. And while there may never be an answer that will get us to a place of forgiveness, perhaps we can begin to see what may have led the perpetrator to commit their crimes.

In a world of *Ubiquitous Relativity*, each person lives in their own universe. This is a somewhat radical statement in favor of the relative nature of things. Throughout history, there have been many brilliant philosophers who have espoused the opposite arguments, in the form of moral universalism. Moral universalism is the position in meta-ethics that some moral values, or a moral system, can be applied universally to everyone (or at least to everyone in similar circumstances). Moral universalism holds that moral values apply to individuals regardless of their personal opinion or the majority opinion of their culture. Other characteristics such as religion, race, or gender are also excluded from moral judgments.[24]

One of the most effective ways to understand *Ubiquitous Relativity* is to compare it to other philosophies. Many of the most respected thinkers over the course of history have stressed some form of universalism. These philosophies feed into our desire for certainty in life. I will discuss these other theories briefly. In no way will this do them justice, but I believe it is important to outline their high-level tenets, so we can put *Ubiquitous Relativity* into context.

Let's start in Classical Greece, during the fifth and fourth centuries B.C. In addition to some of the great military campaigns of this period, like the Battle of Thermopylae (depicted so artfully in Frank Miller's *300*), many of our current-day ideas came from this time in world history. The philosopher Plato lived during this period, and he is widely considered the most pivotal figure in the development of philosophy – especially the Western tradition. Unlike nearly all of his philosophical contemporaries, Plato's entire work is believed to have survived intact for over 2,400 years. He also founded the Academy, the first institution of higher learning in the Western world.

Plato, in some of his writing, espoused a goal-orientated worldview. The aim was to outline how a society might function harmoniously. He considered virtue to be an excellence of the soul. He believed that virtue was a sort of knowledge that is required to reach the ultimate good, or "Eudaimonia."[25]

Plato is one of the oldest known philosophers to espouse universal guidelines to reach an ultimate good. But who defines virtue? Who defines good and evil? In a world of *Ubiquitous Relativity*, there are billions of definitions for those concepts – and it is impossible to paint them all with one brush, as Plato did.

Let's move forward in history to the mid-seventeenth century in England. Does the sentence below sound familiar?

In a natural state people were equal and independent, and everyone had a natural right to defend his Life, Health, Liberty, or Possessions.[26]

Most Americans have heard these words and know they are part of the basis for our democracy. John Locke, one of the most influential political philosophers of the modern period, wrote these words in his Second Treatise on Government. In the Second Treatise on Government, he defended the claim that men are by nature free and equal, against claims that God had made all people naturally subject to a monarch. He argued that people have rights – such as the right to life, liberty, and property – that have a foundation independent of the laws of any particular society.

Locke also made other statements to support a form of universalism. He wrote,

The Bible is one of the greatest blessings bestowed by God on the children of men. It has God for its author; salvation for its end, and truth without any mixture for its matter. It is all pure.

To love our neighbor as ourselves is such a truth for regulating human society, that by that alone one might determine all the cases in social morality.[27]

These statements are interesting in that they make claims about universal ideas, without any regard for a person's culture or lens. He talks about specific rights that include property as independent of any specific culture. But in a world of *Ubiquitous Relativity*, we ask, "What if a culture does not see property in the same

fashion, or does not even know the concept because they are raised in a commu-
nal society?" Locke's statements do not account for these people or their individual
universes. Locke's statement about the Bible implies that this work is universal and
"all pure." What does this mean for people of other religions? How do they fit into
Locke's world? Finally, Locke espouses the Golden Rule, which, as we discussed earlier,
is somewhat flawed.

We continue our journey in time to the mid-eighteenth century. Immanu-
el Kant, a central figure in modern philosophy, was a German philosopher. As he
described in his 1785 work, *Groundwork of the Metaphysics of Morals*, he believed in a
"Categorical Imperative." He defined this to mean:

*Act only according to that maxim by which you can at the same time will
that it should become a universal law.*

Kant suggests that a moral proposition that is true must be one that is absolute
and not tied to any particular conditions, including the identity.[28] This contrasts with
the perspective of *Ubiquitous Relativity*. We view the particular conditions of each
individual as critical for every proposition. Whereas Kant believes one should only act
in ways that one wishes to become universal, in our world of *Ubiquitous Relativity*,
each person cannot define what should or should not become universal law. In fact, we
think that most conflict arises when people believe their actions should become laws
for all people.

We keep moving closer to the present day by examining moral universalism
in some of our modern global institutions. The United Nations adopted the Universal Declaration of Human Rights on December 10, 1948, at the Palais de Chail-
lot. The Declaration represents the first global expression of the rights to which all
human beings are inherently entitled.[29] Although most people would agree that all
humans are entitled to certain rights, the problem comes when people try to identify
these universal rights. What one person in one culture perceives as a universal right
could be interpreted quite differently by someone in another culture. In a world
of *Ubiquitous Relativity*, we question the ability of such global organizations. If I asked
every person on the planet to list five universal rights, could I expect total agreement?

Another philosopher who preached a level of universality in the mid-1900s was
Ayn Rand. In the appendix to her book *Atlas Shrugged*, she says:

*My philosophy, in essence, is the concept of man as a heroic being, with
his own happiness as the moral purpose of his life, with productive
achievement as his noblest activity, and reason as his only absolute.*[30]

Our philosophy of *Ubiquitous Relativity* could not be more different. First, it is not easy to define the word "hero" across cultures – or even across individuals. Some may say that a firefighter rescuing someone from a burning building is a hero because it is literally a life and death situation for anyone unable to escape the fire, while others may say their middle school teacher is a hero because they gave them lessons in life that have formed who they are today. Second, we cannot postulate a moral purpose in life, because each person's universe is different. Some may think happiness is the moral purpose in life, but surely other people and cultures may not value happiness at all. Third, productive achievement is next-to-impossible to define. Who says what an achievement is? Who defines what it means to be productive? Fourth, if reason is our only absolute, how do we define what reason is so that we can apply it in a universal fashion? For all these reasons, this passage from Rand's masterpiece does not seem possible in a world of *Ubiquitous Relativity*.

There are numerous examples of philosophers who espoused different forms of Universalist and Relativist theories. It would be far too arrogant of me – and a direct violation of the world I believe we live in – to declare that I am right or they are wrong. I simply believe that in a world of *Ubiquitous Relativity*, it is difficult to apply absolute standards to almost anything (so, in a perverse way, I am admitting that if most things are relative, so is the philosophy we examine in this book).

I believe humans crave certainty because life is inherently uncertain. We like to make plans and set schedules. We fill out calendars so that we can see how things are supposed to flow over the foreseeable future. We also desire an answer to the biggest question humans have ever asked: "What happens when we die?" For this answer, we typically adopt an ethos and believe that this is the way forward to guarantee a positive present and post-life existence. Many of the religions and philosophers mentioned in this chapter attempt to define universal laws by which we should live. The conundrum is that this planet is home to billions of people with many different belief systems – and most of these belief systems claim to have "the answer" about the "unexplored country" after death.[31]

As followers of these creeds, we inherently believe our system is "right." Otherwise, we may not feel we are living the correct way. It is the certainty we desire that closes us off from others and creates the judgment we seek to reduce in a world of *Ubiquitous Relativity*. We look at other ways of living through the lens of our belief system and judge those lifestyles without any pause whatsoever. If we were to explore other lifestyles and learn about other belief systems, then it might lead us to question our own beliefs – and this engenders uncertainty.

This is why a world of *Ubiquitous Relativity* is outside of our comfort zone. We cannot assume our way is the "right" way and someone else's way is the "wrong" way, because those words rarely apply if each person lives in his or her own universe. So as we begin to analyze the Everlasting Equation, it is perfectly normal if it feels uncomfortable to pause in judgment. For many of us, including myself, it is not a natural state. In some ways, the astronomical pace at which our technology is improving makes it feel even less natural. We explore this phenomenon in the next chapter.

CHAPTER 4

THE FLIPSIDE OF TECHNOLOGY

"It has become appallingly obvious that our technology has exceeded our humanity." [32]

–Albert Einstein

Throughout my journey into a world of *Ubiquitous Relativity*, I frequently asked myself why this philosophy affected me so strongly. Why was I attracted to this new way of thought more and more each day? Why did the concept of *Ubiquitous Relativity* have such a hold of me now, rather than any other time in my years on the planet?

I suspect changing communication patterns may play a part; I have found that I have changed the way I communicate, and so have the people I know. Perhaps we spend too much time on social media or in front of the television. Liberals I know have become more liberal, and conservatives I know have become more conservative. Even more disconcerting is the growing unwillingness of people to even entertain the opposite viewpoint. This unfortunate development is happening quickly. Is the speed of technological innovation the reason?

The irony is that as technological breakthroughs offer us new ways to connect, we have never been more disconnected from one another.

These days in the United States, we seem to constantly remark that we have never seen our country so polarized. Is that really the case, and if so, why is it happening? We have been quick to blame our politicians and the media for driving us to opposite ends of every spectrum. We have used words like "demagoguery" and "divisiveness" to label our leaders and their policies. A concept like polarization feeds on itself, so the more we say it, the more we reinforce its perception. As a student of history, I began to question that description of the current state of our society. What if we are not any more polarized now in our beliefs than we have been in the past? In fact, what if people's beliefs have been far more polarized in other periods of our brief history as a nation?

One only has to study the Civil War to witness the extremes to which people will go in defense of their beliefs. Brothers fought against their own brothers in that conflict. West Point graduates who shared a room while enrolled at the United States Military Academy waged war on each other in the bloodiest of battles. At the time of this writing, we are not seeing the complete fracture of every institution in the country into two separate nations. There is loss of life in this country as a result of conflicting beliefs, but nothing remotely close to the millions of casualties from 1861-1865.[33]

In the late 1960s, violent protests erupted all over the country to end a war in Vietnam that bitterly divided a nation and to fight for the cause of civil rights. The imagery of that era is painful to watch, as Army soldiers killed college students and citizens burned their own draft cards. The riots and marches often grew violent. While we have our share of marches today, they are largely peaceful and without incident.

Putting our era into the perspective of those times in our nation's history causes me to question the conventional wisdom that "we as a country are more polarized than ever."

So if polarization in beliefs has not increased, what has changed recently that makes this feel so much worse than in earlier years? I think there has been a dramatic falloff in our connections to other people – as a direct result of the new technology at our fingertips. This is not to say that technology – which I paint with a very broad brush – has not revolutionized our world in amazing ways. Innovation in life science has increased life expectancy.[34] Mobile handsets and personal computers have allowed us to access all kinds of information from almost anywhere on the planet, enabling more people to learn. New automobile features that rely on increased semiconductor functionality have made it safer to drive. New applications for cellphones have made almost every aspect of our life more efficient, from ridesharing to ordering food to shopping.

Unfortunately, there is a flipside to these huge leaps forward. Our ability to relate to others has deteriorated. This is the paradox I mentioned earlier. The more we develop technology to connect us to people all over the world, the less we require actual human interaction. I don't know exactly when it happened, and perhaps this process has just been like a snowball slowly rolling down a hill and increasing in mass – it starts small and harmless, but then can grow quite dangerous if we lose control.

One can see these changes everywhere in our world. When I walk into any coffee shop in the United States, I see almost every customer working on their laptops while wearing headphones. I cannot tell you how many times I have seen people having dinner together while using their phones instead of having a conversation. Even when we wait in line at the local pharmacy for a prescription or at the local coffee shop for an espresso, we resort to diving into our email instead of diving into a discussion with someone near us. We have the ability to talk via text now, so our audible interactions are decreasing at an alarming rate. Entire families can sit around a breakfast table, each completely engaged in their own electronic device. Dating has become an online activity, and to choose prospective mates we now swipe through digital photographs that can be edited in a multitude of ways.

I am not some old curmudgeon sitting in my rocking chair and complaining that the world has gone to hell in a hand basket since my youth (at least, I tell myself that I'm not). But I have noticed some definite changes in behavior, my own included, that I do not think are for the better. I believe these changes have led to what our civilization perceives as increased polarization.

Before mobile phones, when people said they would meet you somewhere at a certain time, they meant it. They had to mean it because there simply was no way to back out. Now it is so easy to send a text that often there is little to no accountability to keep meetings with other people. This has disconnected us, because making unbreakable commitments kept us tethered to one another.

Before social media, if two people had a disagreement, they discussed it. Their discussion might sometimes be irrational, but nonetheless it happened and it was in person – or at least on a landline with a live voice on the other end of the phone. Now, discussion about issues is limited mostly to online posts and truncated 280-character messages. If we see something on social media we agree with, then we "like" what is said and keep that person as our friend. The opposite is also true. Over the last few years, many times I have heard someone remark, "I just had to 'unfriend' a lot of people because I cannot believe their views." I remember a time when people had wildly divergent beliefs yet could still agree to disagree over a dinner party. At Thanksgiving dinner, it is hard to "unfriend" someone.[35] No matter how irrational the holiday discussions became (my own opinions included), nobody was able to log off from the conversation. Members of families could hold wildly divergent views, but by the nature of actual face-to-face conversation, they had to hear opposing opinions to their own.

When we wall ourselves off from other opinions and thoughts, we only serve to increase our own biases. We lose the opportunity to learn something we did not know

— something which could actually lead to a change in our mindset. We also flat-out lose the chance to influence others. If we are highly convinced of our opinion on a subject, is cutting someone completely out of our lives the best way to try to get them to see our point of view?

Context is pretty clear when people talk face-to-face. I know from someone's body language if something they say is a joke or they are being serious. The inflections in their voice shape my interpretation of their words and sentences. Things are generally not lost in translation, unless we literally speak different languages. Now, much less of our communication takes place in person, and something as simple as a text reply "k" can be interpreted in wildly different ways. If I ask someone a question I think is very important and they respond "k," I could get offended because I was looking for more detail. The person responding with "k" may be simply in a rush. When we communicate through typing to each other, we take away the facial expressions and mannerisms that have been one of our bedrock traits as a species. Without this context, even a common language can seem foreign. Electronic messages are often designed for speed, whereas a handwritten note generally requires more mindfulness and time. Therefore, with new technology comes a degree of thought reduction into our messages to each other.

I will not speak for every culture; however, when I was in Paris, I noticed people sitting outside at cafes, sometimes emotional, sometimes laughing, or sometimes just having a quiet conversation. People were not scrolling through pictures they just took, but simply connecting with one another. The vast amount of wine being drunk and cigarettes being smoked are different issues.

We see videos on social media without context or verification, and we are easily convinced that this in fact accurately represents what actually happened. Technology has made it progressively easier to manipulate news and events, to a point where it can be very difficult to determine the difference between fact and fiction.

I am always surprised at how people in this modern time seemingly would rather keep a memory of something than enjoy it in that specific moment. At concerts, a lot of people film the show with their phones. I suppose this is nice from a nostalgia perspective, but I can watch a video anytime.

When I travel, I am stunned by the number of selfies I see being taken. I find it disconcerting that instead of taking in a beautiful scene with their senses, people would rather take a picture of themselves in the foreground and the image in the background.

On July 17, 2017, the world celebrated its first "Emoji Day."[36] An emoji is a small digital image or icon used to express an emotion or an idea in electronic communication. My wife has one of a woman hitting her forehead in frustration (I seem to get this from her all too frequently).

We are now at a point in human interaction where we have substituted real emotional connection and discussion with electronic images that are already pre-programmed into our phones. This new reality serves to lessen further our actual physical and verbal interactions. Instead of stating how or why I am upset, I can simply select a face with a frown and send it to you. You can choose to ask me why I am upset, or simply reply with a thumbs-down emoji. This type of dialogue becomes so easy that we can have multiple conversations at once yet fail to truly connect during any one of them.

We all search for a balance between the benefits of technologies that allow us to communicate more quickly with others and the importance of vocal and live human connections to form deeper bonds. In a world of *Ubiquitous Relativity*, that balance, which can be evasive at times, is different for everybody. Our instincts are changing as a result of new technologies. Today, many of us default to the ease of electronic forms of communication.

I believe these new traits are also reducing our human connection, which is why it is more important now than ever to appreciate a world of *Ubiquitous Relativity*. So we return to the question: Are we really more polarized now than we have ever been before? Or is it possible we just feel more polarized because we have lost connection to others? There are no easy answers, but I see the pendulum continuing to swing away from actual human contact. I am as guilty as the next person of texting instead of calling someone, but I am trying my best to improve my habits. Our goal is to pause on judgment. When I choose to interact with someone face-to-face or on the phone instead of electronically, I feel I am taking that first step towards that goal. Understanding the Everlasting Equation will illuminate the reasons for pausing on judgment. Let's begin that journey.

PART 2:

The Left Side of the Everlasting Equation

The notion that each individual person senses the universe in a completely unique fashion.

Now that we have discussed many of the factors that brought about *Ubiquitous Relativity* as a new way of seeing the world, we will begin with a brief discussion of how language determines our sense of the world. We will look at each of the five major senses to see how differently we each experience the world on a physiological level. We sometimes forget that there are infinite physical differences between humans. The following discussion will be a reminder of our unique ways of experiencing the world.

Almost all of us exist as part of a group. The group can be as small as our immediate family, or as large as a country, a religion, or people who speak a specific language. If one is immersed solely in this group, then everything encountered outside this group is alien. Our biases and judgments are a product of our own culture, because our views are formulated through this culture since birth. Concepts such as "average" and "normal" vary from society to society and from person to person. This is no surprise, but it is still easy to forget how subtle physiological differences between humans create huge gulfs between our views of the outside world.

As we will see, we can each sense the universe in a manner completely unique to us. The way I see, hear, taste, touch, and smell things is not universal. The goal of this part of our journey is to simply take stock of how differently we each sense the world and to reinforce the fact that these differences truly produce a unique universe for each of us.

CHAPTER 5

LANGUAGE: THE PILLAR THAT HOLDS UP THE LEFT SIDE OF THE EVERLASTING EQUATION

"'Meow' means 'woof' in cat."

— George Carlin[37]

Imagine that people from various countries around the world are hiking through the woods of a forest. At one point on the trail, there is an enormous boulder interrupting the path. Each person must walk left or right around the obstruction to continue on towards their destination. The following words are spray-painted in red on the face of the rock:

Danger is on your left. Safety is on your right.

El peligro está a su izquierda. La seguridad está a su derecha.

Опасность находится слева от вас. Безопасность справа.

危険があなたの左にあります。安全はあなたの右にあります。

Gefahr ist auf der linken Seite. Sicherheit ist auf der rechten Seite.[38]

The fact that this warning message is printed in English, Spanish, Russian, Japanese, and German means that some hikers would see those letters or symbols and immediately know which direction to go to safely continue – but others would have no idea that the choice of direction carries such enormous consequences. People that don't speak any of these languages would have nothing more than a guess or the altruism of another hiker to guide them in their next move.

These barriers of the tongue have been in place since the biblical destruction of the Tower of Babel, when God had quite an issue with humans all speaking the same

26

language.[39] Because our memories are mostly formed through words, language is the beginning of the different ways we sense things. This "declarative memory" is made up of facts and events that can be consciously remembered or "declared" to have happened. It is also described as explicit memory, because its foundation is that this type of memory consists of information that can be explicitly stored and retrieved.[40]

These memories we produce through language begin as soon as we start to speak and think in our native dialect. This type of memory is the memory we experience through most of our lives. Clearly, we cannot overstate the importance of language as a key way people experience the world.

The intricate relationship between language and memory is beyond the scope of this book, but, even without an advanced degree in linguistics or anthropology, I can appreciate the view that language forms our thoughts and helps to create unique universes for the speakers of each language.

The framework for our world of *Ubiquitous Relativity* incorporates some of the controversial ideas around linguistic relativity espoused by Benjamin Whorf and Edward Sapir. Whorf said:

> All the give and take between language and the culture as a whole, wherein is a vast amount that is not linguistic but yet shows the shaping influence of language. In brief, this "thought world" is the microcosm that each man carries about within himself, by which he measures and understands.[41]

Linguistic Relativity as a philosophy has been attributed to Whorf and Sapir. At its most basic, Linguistic Relativity proposes that people who speak one language see the world differently than people who speak another language. Our philosophy of *Ubiquitous Relativity* greatly expands on this concept.

Language allows us to communicate with each other. To survive, a society needs to be able to speak a common jargon. Ever-so-slight nuances can have major consequences when translating from one language to another. It is hard to imagine anything we sense without converting that sensation into words in our mind. Therefore, language dominates the left side of our Everlasting Equation.

In many ways, language is the seed from which all other physiological differences grow. If you look around where you are right now, what do you see? Your eyes literally see the image, but the words that you associate with that image are what matters. Try to imagine a sight without a word attached to it. How would your brain process that imagery?

To put this into perspective, there are nearly seven thousand different languages spoken in the world – so by voice alone, no single person can communicate with everyone else on the planet.[42] Keep this is mind as we explore the widely divergent physical traits we possess as human beings.

We now examine our five senses: Sight, Hearing, Touch, Smell, and Taste. We all have unique abilities and disabilities, and each subtlety frames our perception of the world. The way I sense the world is unlike anyone else's sense of the world.

I will not pretend to understand the reasons for our differences. I merely want to briefly demonstrate that people see, hear, feel, smell, and taste the world differently – and therefore, each person inhabits their own unique universe. So, for the sake of brevity and the full admission of my own limitations in my knowledge of medical conditions, I will focus on some of the most common differences between us. There are many more that are not listed but are fascinating nonetheless. Also, recognize that our age impacts all our senses. It should not be a huge leap of faith to appreciate how eighty-year-olds and eight-year-olds physically sense the world quite differently.

A common effect of any abnormal sense is frustration in daily life. Keep this in mind as we progress through this book. If someone suffers from a condition that impedes their ability to sense the world, it can have a huge impact on their mood and desire to connect with the world around them.

CHAPTER 6

SIGHT / CONDITIONS OF THE EYE

"Eyes are the windows to the soul."[43]

This metaphor is a cliché to say the least, but nevertheless, it posits some relation between what we see and what we feel. As we are dealing with the left side of the Everlasting Equation, the goal is to simply show how we see the world differently.

Most of us are taught from a very young age that normal vision is referred to as "20/20." Simply put, 20/20 means that you can see at twenty feet what you should be able to see at twenty feet. About one out of every three adults have 20/20 vision without glasses, corrective surgery, or contact lenses. In other words, only 35 percent of the population has what is considered "normal" or "perfect" vision. With glasses, surgery, or contacts, approximately 75 percent of adults have 20/20 vision. In infants, depth perception and eye-hand coordination begin to develop around four months after birth. Between four and six months, a baby begins to reach out and touch an object – something that previously only happens by chance. By six months, a child's vision reaches 20/20, which is what we commonly think of as "normal."[44]

We will examine a few of the most prevalent eye conditions that lead us to further question the definition of "normal" vision. These include nearsightedness, farsightedness, color blindness, astigmatism, optical illusions, and how vision of the night sky differs based on the location of the observer.

NEARSIGHTED / FARSIGHTED

Nearsightedness and farsightedness are two of the most frequently identified conditions in our visual ability. Nearsightedness or myopia is when an image is formed in front of the retina instead of on it. This defect can have people seeing closer objects clearly, while distant objects are blurred.[45]

Today, nearly four out of ten Americans have nearsightedness, and this is only expected to grow. By 2050, 50 percent of the world's population – a total of nearly five billion people – will be myopic, according to a study published in the journal *Ophthalmology*.[46] Farsightedness, by contrast, affects about 5 to 10 percent of Americans.[47]

While farsightedness doesn't vary much with age, the same is not true with nearsightedness. Some children lose their 20/20 vision and become nearsighted around age eight or nine. Generally, visual acuity then remains stable throughout life – with perhaps only a slight decrease at the age of sixty or seventy.

Clearly, a person who is farsighted or nearsighted will physically see the world differently than someone who has 20/20 vision. These differences in vision create vast variations in our perception of the world. There is such a significant difference between having 20/20 vision and being nearsighted or farsighted that two people could literally be standing next to each other looking at the same landscape and see highly different versions of the same scene. We will delve into the emotions that these differences can trigger in the next section of this book, but if I can see something beautiful in all its detail and you cannot, surely we will feel differently about what we are witnessing in front of us.

In addition to our ability to see certain objects at different distances, there are other interesting traits we humans have that can distort our visual perception of the universe.

COLOR BLINDNESS

Color blindness (or more accurately, deficiency of color vision) is the decreased ability to see color or differences in color. Out of people with Northern European ancestry, as many as 8 percent of men and 0.5 percent of women have the most common form of red-green color blindness.[48]

One hundred years ago, in 1917, Doctor Shinobu Ishihara introduced an exam which is still the most well-known and popular test for color blindness. His tests consist of a set of colored dotted plates, each showing either a number or a path. These tests are still used by most optometrists and ophthalmologists all around the world.[49]

Imagine that two people walk into the local grocery store. One shopper can see color perfectly and the other customer has color vision deficiency. How would each view the fruits and vegetables? In one universe, it may be easy to determine one fruit from another, but in a colorblind universe it could be incredibly challenging. Imagine how difficult it would be simply to drive on any road with traffic lights without the ability to distinguish one color from another. This would certainly change the way someone views the world and lives life.

ASTIGMATISM

Astigmatism is a common vision problem caused by an error in the shape of the cornea. With this condition, the lens of the eye or the cornea (which is the front surface of the eye) has an irregular curve. This causes blurry, fuzzy, or distorted vision.[50] Approximately 80 percent of Americans have some degree of astigmatism, although many cases do not require correction.[51]

If four out of every five people have abnormal curvature of their eye, then once again, it could mean that people view the same images dissimilarly. If my vision is blurred and often results in headaches, it would make sense that the world I experience is different than the world experienced by someone with "normal" vision.

ILLUSION

Some images are specifically designed to force people to see different things within them. Optical illusions are great examples of this part of *Ubiquitous Relativity*. Optical illusions are caused by the way your eyes and brain work together and are characterized by perceived images that differ from objective reality.

Some clever artistry accentuates the differences in vision among people and always creates a fun debate between them about what they actually see. Optical illusions invite each person to see something different. We examined this in an earlier chapter when we looked at the image of the chalice in conjunction with the two faces. These visual puzzles are designed specifically to take the viewer in different directions. Because these illusions offer multiple images, they can cloud our senses and enhance our focus on finding something each of us can identify. This intensity of thought often leads to an increased feeling of being present. When we look acutely at an optical illusion as we search for a recognizable image, it may help to deemphasize our other senses for those few brief moments. Our other senses can dilute our ability to process the image with our eyes. As a result, we may feel an increased sense of presence during this process.

THE NIGHT SKY / GLOBAL POSITIONING

Additionally, it must be noted that even our position on the planet determines much of what we see. One example is the night sky. Imagine if two people go outside on a clear night and look up at the stars. Will they see the same thing?

In fact, the skies we see are not the same. From any coordinates on earth at any given time, about half of the entire sky is visible. As Earth rotates, the part of the sky that any one person can see will change, unless that person is exactly on the North or South Pole. So, while the sky that someone in Nevada sees overlaps with the sky that someone in Argentina sees, what they see is not the same. For a person in Nevada and a person in Argentina, there is a region of sky that both can see, as well as two regions that only one of them can see. Stars above the North Pole will never be seen by the observer in Argentina, and likewise, stars above the South Pole will never be seen by the observer in Nevada.[52]

There are numerous examples like the night sky, where our physical position on the planet determines what we actually see. Billions of people will see different versions of the night sky, simply because they live in different parts of the planet.

CHAPTER 7

HEARING / CONDITIONS OF
THE EAR

"If a tree falls in a forest and no one is around to hear it, does it make a sound?" [53]

This philosophical and scientific question is one of the most famous questions asked over the years. I do not know the answer, but I am certain that our hearing ability has been key to our survival since the dawn of humanity. From the resonance of predators approaching to the sound of enemy combatants, our ears have been critical in our evolution. We can hear water flowing through the woods, the cries of a baby, and car horns. That being said, it is stunning to think about the multitude of differences in our auditory perception. Let's look at a few examples of different hearing conditions that can completely change our perception of what is around us and what our world sounds like.

As with vision, there is a "normal" level of hearing. Individual hearing ability is quantified in decibels relative to this normal hearing level, with higher numbers of decibels indicating worse hearing. Normal hearing is measured as less than twenty-five decibels in adults and less than fifteen decibels in children.[54] Approximately 15 percent of American adults aged eighteen and over report some trouble hearing,[55] and this effect increases dramatically with age – in fact, more than 25 percent of Americans older than sixty-five have disabling hearing loss.[56]

As we can see, hearing varies from person to person, and this variation has a dramatic effect on our lives. We will look at a handful of the conditions that affect our sense of sound. These include tinnitus, the difference between our right and left ear, how a gift for music may change what we hear, and vertigo. Almost any experience, from hearing the dialogue during a movie, to listening to music, to the sound of one's own voice are all dependent on our ability to hear. Would going to a Broadway show feel the same for someone who has lost 50 percent of their hearing as it would for a person who has their hearing function intact? In the second part of this book we will take a deeper look at the emotions these differences in hearing may evoke, but I would imagine that going to a child's music recital would impact the emotions of people with different hearing abilities in rather different ways.

TINNITUS

Tinnitus (pronounced ti-ni-tis), or ringing in the ears, is the sensation of hearing all kinds of sounds, including ringing, hissing, chirping, buzzing, and whistling. The noise can be intermittent or all the time, and its volume can vary. It is often worse when background noise is low, so those who suffer from this condition may be most aware of it at night when they are attempting to fall asleep in a quiet room.[57]

Imagine how different the world must sound for people with this condition. Millions of Americans (including myself) suffer from tinnitus, often to a debilitating degree, and it is one of the most common health conditions in the country. Almost 15 percent of the population experience some form of tinnitus. Eight percent of the population have chronic tinnitus, while 1 percent have extreme and debilitating cases.[58]

I cannot hear high-pitched sounds, and it is hard to hear what is coming from behind my left ear (the source of the ringing). This was collateral damage from firing assault rifles on a range in Korea. Therefore, I am largely unaware of what is just behind my left shoulder. I am often embarrassed when someone walking behind me has to say "excuse me" multiple times before it is audible to me. It is hard to explain to them that I literally could not hear them, and that I am not intentionally trying to be rude (my wife swears I use this to my advantage when she has asked me to do something, and I claim I didn't hear.)

I adjust to this impediment; to hear words clearly, I have to lean into many conversations with my right ear. I need some level of white noise when I sleep, because the ringing gets quite loud in the dead of night. Imagine a couple sleeping, where one has this condition and the other has perfect hearing. I remember how I heard the world before this condition, and I know how the world sounds today. My surroundings are different for me now; it is hard to be a part of conversations in loud atmospheres, and as a result, I lose some human contact.

PRESBYCUSIS

Age-related hearing loss, or "presbycusis," is the slow loss of hearing that happens as people age. Tiny hair cells inside the inner ear help you to hear. These cells pick up sound waves and change them into the nerve signals that the brain interprets as sound. Hearing loss takes place when the tiny hair cells are damaged or die. The hair cells do not regenerate, so most hearing loss caused by this kind of damage is permanent.[59]

Like other senses, a six-year-old child and a seventy-five-year-old man walking down the street in New York City would probably have drastically different hearing experiences.

RIGHT VS. LEFT EAR

Imagine a huge lecture hall where hundreds of students are taking a course on English as a second language. For the entirety of the yearlong course, the students do not change seats. One group of students sits on the far left of the auditorium and hears most of the instructions out of their right ears. Another group sits on the far right side of the lecture hall and hears the teacher speak mostly through their left ears. Does it make a difference in their ability to learn English?

Some scientists believe that we do hear things differently out of each ear. It may have something to do with the way our skulls are shaped and the variations in individual bone structures. When a sound bounces off the structures of the inner ear, it reflects off the ear and the bones in the head. According to the Acoustical Society of America, a small difference in shape and bone density can engender a huge difference in the vibrations that we ultimately hear. Female skulls tend to vibrate faster than the skulls of the male, and each person's recorded vibrations can vary between as much as thirty-five to sixty-five hertz. That's a large range, and it's been connected to which sounds we find pleasurable or distasteful. Your right ear may be more efficient than your left ear at receiving sounds from speech, whereas your left ear is more sensitive to sounds of music, according to American researchers who studied the hearing of three thousand newborns. It has long been known that the right and left halves of the brain register sounds differently because of differences in the brain cells in each side – but the results from the study indicate that the ears play a much more important role than previously believed.[60]

MUSICAL SKILL

Do musicians hear the world differently from non-musicians? In one study, each group was asked to pick out certain voices from a noisy room, and musicians tended to hear them while non-musicians tended not to. In fact, several studies have demonstrated that the entire auditory system of a musician is physically different. Signals that help with appreciating tone and pitch are much stronger when they travel through a musician's brain than through the brain of a non-musician. The differences in how we process sound might explain why we love or hate certain kinds of music. If someone has an ear for music and can pick up the sound of pleasant melodies in a noisy room, then it may improve their ability to relax and concentrate even while non-musicians find it hard to focus. Off-key sounds, on the other hand, may not give musicians an edge compared to non-musicians.[61]

VERTIGO

Vertigo is an inner ear condition that causes sufferers to feel off-balance. If a person suffers from vertigo, they might feel like they are spinning or that the world around them is spinning.[62]

About 30 percent of people over the age of sixty-five experience dizziness or other issues with balance as a result of vertigo. Twelve percent of those who suffer from vertigo live with chronic dizziness, and 33 percent live with chronic balance issues. Even simple tasks can be extremely difficult to perform for those with vertigo.[63] Vertigo sufferers need extra time in accomplishing almost any task and usually need to be under some kind of supervision. In extreme cases, the most basic pleasures of life, from walking in the woods to running in the park, become nearly impossible for them to experience.

CHAPTER 8

TOUCH / CONDITIONS OF THE SKIN

"Never touch your idols: the gilding will stick to your fingers."[64]

–Gustave Flaubert, Madame Bovary

Before I started researching for this book, I assumed that the sense of touch did not vary much between people. But like most things in a world of *Ubiquitous Relativity*, I simply had not learned enough about the subject. There are, in fact, great variations in the way each of us touches the world.

The combinations of genes, cells, and neural circuits that form the sense of touch have been crucial in our evolution; for example, we knew to avoid fire because it burned our skin. The human brain has grown to have two distinct but parallel pathways for processing touch information. We will look at a few of the most common disorders of the sense of touch and conditions of the skin: tactile defensiveness, tactile hyposensitivity, and psoriasis.[65]

TACTILE DEFENSIVENESS

One of the most common disorders of touch is tactile defensiveness. People with this condition have markedly diminished tolerance for any touch sensations. Although some adults experience tactile defensiveness, it generally manifests in children. The Children's Academy for Neurodevelopment and Learning explains that incoming stimuli are not processed correctly in the brain, causing the child to register even mild sensory input as extreme, irritating, or even painful.[66]

TACTILE HYPOSENSITIVITY

Tactile hyposensitivity is the opposite of tactile defensiveness. Those with this disorder of touch have diminished tactile stimulation. This can result in injury, because the threshold for pain is often quite high. Those with this disorder may gravitate toward experiences of high sensation in order to feel. They may love extremes in surface conditions, including those that provide lots of texture and stimulation, and may seek out messy, loud activities.[67]

I wonder if this may explain why some people are able to walk on hot coals or live in extremely cold climates, whereas this is not possible for many others.

PSORIASIS

Psoriasis is a chronic inflammatory disease of the immune system. It mostly affects the skin and joints, but it also may affect the fingernails, the toenails, and the inside of the mouth. Psoriasis-affected sections of skin look red, raised, and have silvery-white, scaly flakes. These patches usually show up on the scalp, elbows, knees, and lower back.[68] In a society like ours in the United States, which is extremely focused on outward appearance, perhaps having this condition would decrease someone's desire to be out in public.

Would this then limit their ability to connect with others? Roughly 7.5 million people in the United States have psoriasis. This condition occurs in people of all ages but is primarily seen in adults.[69]

CHAPTER 9

SMELL / CONDITIONS OF THE NOSE

"Our foyer has a funny smell that doesn't smell like anyplace else. I don't know what the hell it is. It isn't cauliflower and it isn't perfume—I don't know what the hell it is—but you always know you're home."[70]

– J.D. Salinger

So how exactly does the human sense of smell work? When odors enter the nose, they travel to the top of the nasal cavity to the olfactory cleft where the nerves for smell are located.[71]

Five percent of our DNA is devoted to olfaction. Although scientists used to think that the human nose could identify about ten thousand different smells, it is likely that people can identify far more scents. In fact, some estimate that the average person can detect at least one trillion different smells – a far cry from the previous estimate of ten thousand.[72]

There appears to be a difference between the sexes when it comes to the sense of smell. Women have more cells in the olfactory bulb, with 16.2 million cells total in the average female olfactory bulb but only 9.2 million total cells in the average male olfactory bulb.[73] Would a woman and a man smell the scent of a garden the same way? These differences could lead to conflict; for example, a wife may get frustrated with her husband because he does not want to spend as much time with her in the garden because the pleasurable scents aren't as strong for him.

We now examine three disabilities of the sense of smell: hyposmia, anosmia and sleep apnea.

HYPOSMIA AND ANOSMIA

Hyposmia, which affects approximately four million Americans, is a reduced sense of smell.[74] Anosmia, an extreme form of this ailment, is the inability to perceive

39

odor or the loss of the sense of smell. Anosmia may be temporary, but some anosmia can be permanent.[75]

Clearly, someone with hyposmia or anosmia experiences a different world than someone with a fully functioning sense of smell – and by the estimates above, roughly one out of every one hundred people have little to no sense of smell.

Problems with the sense of smell increase as people get older, and these problems are more common in men than women. One study found that nearly 25 percent of men ages sixty to sixty-nine have a smell disorder, while about 11 percent of women in that age range reported a problem.[76]

SLEEP APNEA

Sleep apnea is a common disorder in which people have pauses in breathing or shallow breaths while they sleep. Breathing pauses can last from a few seconds to minutes, and they may occur thirty times or more an hour. Sleep apnea is usually a chronic condition that disrupts sleep. When a sleeping person's breathing pauses or becomes shallow, they often move out of deep sleep and into light sleep. As a result, the quality of their sleep is poor, which makes them tired during the day.[77] This condition of the nose can be caused by nasal obstruction – which encompasses anything which hinders the airflow in and out of the nose affecting one or both nasal passages. Nasal obstruction is usually caused by either swelling of the nasal tissue or an anatomical blockage that results in a narrowing of the nasal cavity and the feeling of the passages being congested.[78]

Most people have some sort of imbalance in the size of their breathing passages. In fact, estimates indicate that 80 percent of people (most of them unknowingly) have some sort of misalignment to their nasal septum.[79] I know exactly how different the world must seem to someone with sleep apnea and someone without the condition. I had sleep apnea due to a deviated septum and was waking up all the time in the middle of the night. (As you can imagine, it was not endearing to my wife.) I have since had corrective surgery, and now I can sleep normally – and the difference has had a profound impact on me. My sense of smell is more acute now and my general mood has improved. Furthermore, had it not been for that surgery, and my encounter at the stoplight with the woman in the car next to me, I may not have written this book.

CHAPTER 10

TASTE / CONDITIONS OF
THE TONGUE

"My tastes are simple: I am easily satisfied with the best."[80]

–Winston Churchill

Finally, we look at our sense of taste – and I don't mean a sense of fashion, because then I would certainly serve as an example of someone with a disorder. About half of the sensory cells on our tongue react to several of the five basic tastes. These cells differ only in their varying levels of sensitivity to the different basic tastes. Each cell has a specific palette of tastes with fixed rankings. This means that a particular cell might be most sensitive to sweet, followed by sour, salty and bitter – while another cell has its own ranking.

The full experience of a flavor is produced only after all of the sensory cell profiles from the different parts of the tongue are combined. The other half of the sensory cells and nerve fibers are specialized to react to only one taste. These cells transmit information on the intensity of the stimulus – how salty or sour something tastes. We can taste close to one hundred thousand different flavors. When we combine our sense of taste with the senses of touch, temperature, and smell, there are an enormous number of different possible flavors. Like the rest of our senses, our ability to taste can be affected by various medical conditions. Conditions that affect taste include phantom taste, hypogeusia, and dysgeusia.[81]

PHANTOM TASTE / HYPOGEUSIA / DYSGEUSIA

The most common taste disorder is phantom taste perception, which is a lingering, often unpleasant taste, which someone might experience even when they have nothing in their mouth.

Another type of taste disorder is hypogeusia, a reduced ability to taste sweet, sour, bitter, salty, and savory (umami). Ageusia, which is rare, is the inability to detect any tastes. Dysgeusia is a condition in which a foul, salty, rancid, or metallic taste sensation persists in the mouth.

More than two hundred thousand people visit a doctor each year for problems with their ability to taste or smell. Scientists believe that up to 15 percent of adults might have a taste or smell problem, but many don't seek a doctor's help.[82]

Imagine two people are eating an exquisite meal at a five-star restaurant and they agree to each have the identical seven-course tasting menu. One has a normal sense of taste and one suffers from dysgeusia. Will both have the same experience as they eat the same foods in the same order? Will both people feel that it was worth the money for the dinner?

Chapter 11

CONDITIONS INCLUSIVE OF ALL FIVE SENSES

"The only time you really live fully is from thirty to sixty. The young are slaves to dreams; the old servants of regrets. Only the middle-aged have all their five senses in the keeping of their wits." [83]

–Hervey Allen

There are other interesting human conditions that combine various senses. We will examine synesthesia, insomnia, and autism. These last two are quite common and significantly impact the way people with those disorders sense the world.

SYNESTHESIA

Synesthesia is a neurological phenomenon in which stimulation of one sensory or cognitive pathway leads to automatic, involuntary experiences in a second sensory or cognitive pathway. People who report a lifelong history of such experiences are known as "synesthetes." They may see sounds, taste words, or feel a sensation on their skin when they smell certain scents. They may also see abstract concepts like time projected in the space around them. Scientists used to think synesthesia was quite rare, but now it is believed that up to 4 percent of the population has some form of the condition. [84]

Children without synesthesia are often critical of a synesthete's descriptions of the world, and may conclude those experiences are alien. When encountering new people, a person with sound-color synesthesia may be naturally drawn to someone with a "pretty" voice, while avoiding those with "sharp" or "glaring" voices. [85]

INSOMNIA

People with insomnia can feel dissatisfied with their sleep and usually experience one or more of the following symptoms: fatigue, low energy, difficulty concentrating, mood disturbances, and decreased performance in work or at school. Insomnia is a common sleep problem for adults. The National Institutes of Health estimates that roughly 30 percent of the general population complains of sleep disruption, and approximately 10 percent have associated symptoms of daytime functional impairment consistent with the diagnosis of insomnia.[86]

Someone who suffers from insomnia likely experiences the world differently than someone who gets a full night's sleep. If one person has mood changes because of insomnia, and another person does not, then it is quite possible they approach others in life and the opportunity for human connections completely differently.

First and foremost, total sleep deprivation impairs attention and working memory, but it also affects other functions, such as long-term memory and decision-making. It is believed that visual tasks are especially vulnerable to sleep loss because iconic memory (a type of sensory memory that lasts very briefly before quickly fading) is weakened with insomnia.[87]

AUTISM

Autism is a lifelong developmental disability that affects how a person communicates and interacts with other people, and how they experience the world around them.[88] Currently, about one out of every sixty-eight children in the United States has autism. There are varying degrees of autism, and each carries with it a unique way of sensing the universe.[89]

This disability can impact each of the five senses to different degrees depending on the severity of autism. Central vision can be blurry, depth perception is at times poor, and images may fragment. Someone with autism may only hear sounds in one ear or have difficulty cutting out background noise. Smells can be intense and overpowering. Certain textures cause discomfort – so someone with autism may only be comfortable eating smooth foods like mashed potatoes or ice cream. Touch can be painful and uncomfortable – so someone with autism may not like to be touched, which can affect their relationships with others.[90]

CONCLUSION ON THE LEFT SIDE OF THE EVERLASTING EQUATION

When all these different conditions across all of our senses are considered, we see the validity of the left side of our Everlasting Equation – we see that each person senses the universe in a unique fashion. Try to imagine what it would be like to have a different sense of sight or smell than your own. It is nearly impossible. We can try on other people's glasses to change our vision, or cover our ears to see what it might be like to have reduced hearing, but rarely do we get any realistic idea of how they feel. This is a crucial point. If we are willing to acknowledge that we cannot fully understand how other people sense the world, then we can begin to understand why different people experience life through their own universes. They may walk side by side with us on a street and have a completely different physiological experience. They may hear different sounds than you hear, they may smell different scents, and they may see different colors.

As we have seen, the frustration that comes along with diminished or abnormal senses has a direct effect on our emotions and ability to connect with other people. Imagine how someone who has very bad hearing would feel at a loud dinner party. Perhaps they remain silent and feel disconnected, because they cannot understand what anyone is saying. Perhaps someone who is color blind will be less excited about going out into nature with a group of people, because they cannot enjoy the same contrasts in color as the others. I often dismiss people as anti-social when they withdraw from many activities, although I have no idea if they suffer from any kind of sensory deprivation. I do not even consider how difficult and frustrating it must be for them to enjoy sensations that I take for granted.

Now that we have examined how we truly don't know how others sense the universe, we can take the next steps down the road to a world of *Ubiquitous Relativity*. We now address the second part of the Everlasting Equation and take a look at how variation in senses triggers an infinite amount of different emotional responses.

PART 3:

The Right Side of the Everlasting Equation

Each individual's reaction to those senses is a direct result of unique experiences over the course of a lifetime.

In the second part of this book, we considered how our ways of sensing the world differ physiologically. But how and why do these senses trigger our emotions? These answers truly get to the crux of what it means to exist in a world of *Ubiquitous Relativity*. We internally process what we sense externally – and that is part of our essence as a human being.

Rene Descartes famously said, "I think, therefore I am."[91] Our philosophy, by contrast, says, "I unthink, therefore I am." This is a change of only two letters from Descartes' mantra, but it suggests a completely different way of living. Descartes implies that our existence is a result of our thought, whereas I propose fuller lives are a result of challenging all our beliefs.

Some may say this is simply a case of semantics, and perhaps that's valid. We have spent our entire lives in thought. Like many others, I always believed that most of my thoughts were rational and should therefore dictate some kind of universal standard. As I thought about all that I had learned over the course of my lifetime, I preached to anyone who would listen (and some who wouldn't) about how my facts and experiences were the right ones. Essentially, I was arguing that "I think, therefore everyone is." This mode of living was easy and comfortable for me, and I stuck to my biases and prejudices and never once truly challenged my own judgments.

So what does it mean to unthink something? Essentially, it means we take our first judgments of everything we sense around us and question our conclusions. We have learned to think and react to the world through our own lens and within the confines of our own universe. So as we look at the other universes around us, we may attempt the difficult task of beginning to retrain our mind to question these judgments. This is no short order.

For most of my life, it never occurred to me that my thoughts were only a window into my experiences (and mine alone). This is what we mean in the Everlasting Equation when we use the word "unique." After the series of personal experiences I described in the introduction to this book, I began to see how my judgments and thoughts drove most of my existence. In this part of our book, we will look at how we sense things and then quickly make judgments despite knowing almost nothing about the person, place, or thing we are judging.

Rather than simply demonstrate individual responses to senses in isolation, I think it is more appropriate to look at emotions we feel in relation to others. This is best seen through interaction with multiple people. We inhabit a world of 7.5 billion people – so these inputs and reactions occur hundreds of times a day, are largely unavoidable, and affect us in ways we do not even realize. In turn, the emotional responses we have to our senses are a direct result of every cumulative experience throughout the totalities of our lives. In the next chapters, I have created some scenarios that illustrate this dynamic and show how we regularly miss opportunities to connect with people. These missed opportunities occur because we extrapolate past experiences and biases to interactions in the present moment. As the Everlasting Equation indicates, there are infinite potential examples of this phenomenon.

Each of the scenarios discussed in this portion of the book describe everyday encounters. We will observe multiple people within these encounters and watch for different sensory inputs, prejudgments, and emotional responses. We have all probably felt similar emotions to each person in each scenario. The goal is to further appreciate the things we do not know about a situation – before we judge it. We will see how many times we fail to appreciate the other universes around us. Within the description of each viewpoint or person in the scenarios, we can further recognize that we live in a world of *Ubiquitous Relativity*.

The one certainty in each situation is that the more people we add to the encounter, the more likely we are to increase judgment and miss opportunities for human connection – and human connection is really the ultimate goal. There is an opportunity cost to each judgment, and this is inherently different from a monetary cost.

A monetary cost can often be measured, whereas an opportunity cost cannot be easily calculated. Opportunity cost is the loss of potential gain from other alternatives when one alternative is chosen.[92] For instance, if I am deciding whether or not I should take a vacation, I know the real cost of the flights and the hotels – so if I go, I know what money I will spend, and if I do not go on the trip, I know what money I will save. If I decide to forego the vacation, I cannot measure the cost of the experiences like surfing or relaxation that I will lose. This is the opportunity cost of not taking the vacation. When I choose to reject a person due to one of my biases, I lose out on the opportunity for a connection.

I often look at my life as I would a ledger or balance sheet. I view some people as assets and some as liabilities, and I consider the real cost of each relationship. I have always looked at my relationships and concluded that some add to my life and some subtract from it – but that is an oversimplified way of viewing each of these relationships. The opportunity costs of my life can be significant because they are a direct result of my judgments. That cost can be best expressed as the sum total of the missed true connections to other people. If I choose to dismiss other people without any reason other than my own emotional reactions, then I have allowed my judgments to cost me potentially deep personal relationships. This is not to say that I might have a deep relationship with every person I interact with. It simply suggests that I could have real connections with some of those people I pass over every day because of my biases. Judgment is what leads each of our universes to collide violently with one another. As such, a pause on this instinct can lead us to coexist with other universes through mutual respect and understanding.

In each of the vignettes in this section of the book, try to identify these opportunity costs. What potential deep connections do the participants lose as a result of their biases? Where do their assumptions lead towards conflict and away from harmony? The beauty is that each new situation throughout our lives affords us the chance for new human connections.

It is critical that we share details of our own universe with others when given the opportunity. If we are asked why we feel a certain way or believe a certain idea, it may help to answer the question. By opening up our own universe, we may create another chance at a human connection. In each scenario, we will also look at what some of the players could have done to open their universes to others and thus help to avoid conflict or judgment.

In totality, each of the short scenarios in this part of the book is an opportunity to see the dynamic world of *Ubiquitous Relativity.*

CHAPTER 12

WHAT DOES IT MEAN TO BE OLD OR YOUNG?

"I am not young enough to know everything."[93]

–J. M. Barrie

The definition of what it means to be old or young has been debated since the beginning of time. Each culture has its own perspective on the subject and treats its citizens differently based on age. Many societies provide a social safety net for its older people once they reach a certain age.

On a basic level, life expectancy can be used as a measuring stick for how age determines what it means to be "young" or "old" in each civilization. As we look at the right side of the Everlasting Equation through the following scenario, we need to consider the extreme influence of culture in forming age-related biases.

Three men huddle around a chessboard in a poorly maintained park in Brooklyn, New York. It is late October, so the sky has exchanged its long blue days for short gray ones. The few remaining trees have started discarding their leaves towards the concrete and hard dirt below. Other groups of unlikely friends occupy adjacent chessboards as nannies push sleeping children in strollers along uneven asphalt paths.

The men differ in every aspect except their love for the game of chess. The first of them is a forty-year-old Japanese man, Haruto, who moved to the United States four years ago. Haruto speaks English well enough by most standards and fluently by the standards of New York City. Haruto is very close with his family, including his ninety-five-year-old grandfather, who still is healthy and active.

The second man is Gabriel, a thirty-year-old from Sierra Leone. He has been in this country for only two years, and speaks English fluently with a strong accent. Gabriel is single and both of his parents died a few years ago.

The third man is Billy, a seventy-year-old American from Youngtown, Ohio. He is retired after a lifetime of toiling from an assembly line to a middle-management position in an auto parts company.

The cool sixty-degree temperature reminds the three friends that the days of their outdoor chess games may be nearing their end for the year. Haruto does not seem to mind much. Billy has felt seventy years of autumn days, although his skin gets much colder now than it used to this time of the year. Gabriel shivers, as his body is still adjusting to the dramatic climate changes of New York.

Billy looks up from the chessboard while thinking of his next move and says to his friends, "Youth is truly wasted on the young. I swear, it takes me an extra five minutes just to get out of bed these days. I never knew I could be so sore from walking a mile. Thank goodness for aspirin." As Billy is talking, the other men can see the deep canyons of wrinkles on his forehead. Every day, they see the dark purple of his hands as he moves the pieces around the board.

Haruto, who is staring at his white bishop and contemplating his next move, looks up at his American friend and says, "You are a young man still with plenty of life left in you. Do not dwell on what you do not have. Focus on the fact that you can still walk a mile, and tomorrow aim for a mile and a quarter."

Gabriel observes the chess match from his perch on the top rails of a nearby park bench. He hears their comments and directs his eyes towards Billy. "You have lived quite a long life already and you should be grateful for every additional day you have on this planet. If it means you have to rest more, then so be it."

According to this brief exchange, Billy is both a young and an old man.[94] Who is right and who is wrong? Upon further thought, one can see the rationale for the different viewpoints of Haruto and Gabriel. After all, the life expectancy in Sierra Leone is just over fifty, while in Japan, the life expectancy is nearly eighty-five. All three men are friends who see each other every morning for these mental competitions and conversations. Nobody questions the motives of anyone else, and the conversation goes on without incident.

Now imagine a scenario where these same three men do not know each other. Instead, imagine that Billy, Haruto, and Gabriel are playing separate chess games in the Brooklyn park. The children from the local elementary school come into the park during recess at 12:00 p.m. The screaming and yelling of young children tends to cloud the strategy of the quiet thoughtful minds, so this is usually the impetus for the chess players to call it a day. The men pack up the chessboards and exit the park in the same direction. Billy, Haruto, and Gabriel have all seen each other in the park before, but they do not know each other by name. Haruto and Gabriel notice Billy moving slowly and grimacing with each step. They see his weathered hands hold the railing as he walks down the stairs to the platform. The doors open and all three men enter the uptown train. There is one open seat in their car, and Gabriel looks at Billy and motions for the older man to take the seat. Before Billy can even lift his hand off the center pole, Haruto bolts into the seat and starts reading the newspaper.

Gabriel hears the sound of the subway screeching and clawing its way up the track. The interval of quiet groaning and piercing sound irritates him. He then looks at the pole he is grasping for balance and sees the fingerprints of countless others who previously had pressed their hands on the metal. Gabriel does his best to avoid germs, and the sight of fresh palm prints around his hand make him anxious.

Gabriel is taken aback and quite angry that the Japanese man showed no deference or respect for the older American man. In Sierra Leone, a man who is seventy is to be revered and respected, because he has far outlived the average person. So when Haruto disregarded Billy, Gabriel saw it as an affront. Remember, the average life expectancy in Japan is almost eighty-five years old – so for Haruto, this was not necessarily a show of disrespect. A seventy-year-old man is still considered quite young in his culture. Gabriel turns to Billy and says, "That gentleman is quite rude for taking the seat from you. It amazes me that certain types of people have no manners." Billy just nods and shrugs his shoulders.

So here we have a situation where the man from Sierra Leone judged the Japanese man using the cultural norms of his universe – in other words, assuming that what is considered right in his culture is the right way of doing things for every culture. Gabriel might form an opinion of all Japanese men based on this one action, all the while not considering that Haruto has his own cultural biases that render his action totally ordinary to him.

We ask once more: is there a right or wrong here? Or is this simply a world of *Ubiquitous Relativity*, where emotions related to senses lead to completely different conclusions, with none more right than the others? Both Haruto and Gabriel see Billy. But the sight of the American's age triggers completely different emotional responses in each of them, leading to judgment and misunderstanding of the ensuing actions. Gabriel is already agitated by the cold temperatures outside, the sounds of the subway, and the clammy pole he is holding in the train. These senses of sound and touch exacerbate his hasty judgment of Haruto. Gabriel may choose to harbor resentment towards Haruto, thus losing any opportunity to eventually form a friendship. Perhaps they have much in common, as both are somewhat recent immigrants to this country.

As we can see, there is an opportunity cost to applying the ethos of our universe to all the other universes with which we come into contact. The opportunity cost in this case is a potential human bond that was jettisoned by a judgment. At any point after Haruto jumped into the empty seat, Gabriel could have asked himself, "Why might this man have jumped into this seat, when I view his action as clearly disrespectful?" There are many answers to this question. If nothing else, Gabriel would be pausing for a moment and considering how his judgment could be wrong. It is even possible that Gabriel would entertain inviting Haruto to play chess.

CHAPTER 13

LIFE IS SHORT, LIFE IS LONG

"It's evolution, baby."[95]

— Eddie Vedder

Some people see life as long; they see it as an opportunity for each person to have a lasting effect on civilization. Others view life as short; they see us as simply moving through our years, with limited impact in the grand scheme of things. But have we ever thought that both of these contrasting perspectives could be right? Could our quick judgment, based on our own bias, neglect the fact that the person espousing the opposite viewpoint has legitimate reasons for their beliefs? Religion and the debate between creationists and evolutionists seem to bring out some of the strongest and most unyielding opinions. This harkens back to our discussion of certainty earlier in this book. As we will see in the following scenario, many people have different opinions on what happens when we die and on how to live to ensure something good awaits at the end of our existence on this planet.

Yawns ricochet around a train cabin as the morning sun rises. Jimmy and Trent, good friends from college, are seated next to each other. They are traveling home from the funeral of their friend Amy, who died at the age of forty-five. Both men remain quiet for a while (as so few people do when there is not much to say).

Jimmy hails from an evangelical family and adheres strictly to the Bible. A large crucifix on a golden chain hangs outside his t-shirt. He sits on the seat closest to the window and sees the sunlight begin to wrap around his world. He smiles and says, "Amy had a good life and made a difference in the lives of many people in just a short period of time. She was someone I could count on. Whenever I needed advice on how to be a better person, she was the first friend I called. I know sometimes our society thinks everyone should live much longer, but living until forty-five still is a lengthy

53

amount of time.

Trent, an atheist who grew up in a household of evolutionists, responds, "I don't know, Jimmy. Forty-five is pretty young. We need every year we can get to be able to truly impact a world as old as ours. I think she was taken from us before her time."

Since Jimmy and Trent have known each other for a while, they agree to disagree without saying another word. Instead, they silently reflect on how much they miss their mutual friend.

Elizabeth, a forty-five-year-old woman who grew up in an agnostic household, sits across the aisle from the two men and listens to their conversation. The sunlight has not found its way to where she is seated, so she is surrounded only by dim light. She sips her coffee, because it is still chilly in the cabin. After hearing Jimmy's opinion on what it means to live a long time, Elizabeth reflects on her own life. She feels incredibly young and believes a full time on earth should last well into one's seventies. Recently, she tore her ACL and her orthopedist told her that "she needs to realize she is not twenty-five anymore."

"What kind of a man thinks forty-five years is a full life?" she wonders. She sees his necklace with the cross hanging out over his shirt and thinks to herself, "Figures. A Bible thumper." She glares at Jimmy until their eyes meet, and she shakes her head disapprovingly at him. The train rumbles on down the track.

Who is right in this scenario? Can only one of them be correct? There are many interesting aspects to Jimmy and Trent's conversation and the ensuing interaction between Elizabeth and Jimmy. First, we have the concept of a human life in relation to the history of the world. Because creationists and evolutionists disagree on the planet's age, this enormous difference affects how one looks at time in general.

Mathematically, we can think of Amy's age at death (forty-five years) as the numerator in this case, and we can think of the age of the planet as the denominator. A creationist may view Amy's life as forty-five years out of a total of six thousand.[96] An evolutionist, by contrast, may view Amy's life as forty-five years out of a total of four and a half billion.[97] As these ratios show, there is a massive difference between the ways a creationist and an evolutionist might view the length of a life relative to the age of the planet.

The second aspect of note is that both Jimmy and Trent are quick to drop their debate and think of Amy, because they know each other and their differences do not damage what ties them together. They have an existing human connection that is a result of learning about each other's universes.

The third aspect illustrates how we live in a world of *Ubiquitous Relativity*. Elizabeth doesn't know either Jimmy or Trent, but she has her own views based on her current physiological and emotional states. She is especially sensitive to the issue of age this morning, because of her doctor's recent admonishment to not train like she is twenty years younger. Also, she is cold in the cabin, which impacts the way she feels.

Elizabeth has disdain for Jimmy because she does not agree with his views, and the symbol of the cross he wears adds to her anger. She does not know that Jimmy was taught from birth that the world was only six thousand years old. So we are left to wonder, would things have been different if Elizabeth realized that Jimmy was framing things through the belief system he knows? With regards to opportunity cost, did Elizabeth miss out on a potential connection with Jimmy because she assumed that the laws of her universe were the "right" laws? Wouldn't it have been interesting if, instead of glaring at him, Elizabeth asked him why he believed forty-five years was a long time?

We know so very little about the other universes around us. The only way to learn anything about them is to connect. The more we pause on judgment, the more opportunities there are to connect with the people all around us on this planet.

CHAPTER 14

PATRIOTISM AND THE POWER
OF SYMBOLS

"A soldier will fight long and hard for a bit of colored ribbon."[98]

–Napoleon Bonaparte

Two people can see the same image and have completely different responses with different degrees of intensity. One of the greatest examples of the intensity of emotions is the reaction to seeing a flag.

Millions of people have died over the years for a cause often represented by a pennant. U.S. Civil War soldiers placed great importance on the flags of their regiments, and men would sacrifice their lives defending a regimental flag to protect it from capture by the enemy.

People have even attempted to put "The Flag Desecration Amendment" (often referred to as the Flag-Burning Amendment) into permanent law as a constitutional amendment to the Bill of Rights. This would allow the government to prohibit and punish citizens for physically desecrating the flag of the United States.[99]

Many citizens argue that freedom of speech protects people who choose to burn the flag; they claim that the best thing about this country is that we have the right to free expression. The concept of flag desecration continues to provoke a heated debate over the value of protecting a symbol versus preserving free speech. Some flags, like the Nazi flag or the Confederate flag, evoke tremendous emotion given their roles throughout history up to and including the present day.

In the United States, we even have a national holiday just for the flag. One governor recently said:

> On the 101st anniversary of Flag Day, we recognize our American flag
> that defines the unity and prosperity of our great nation. Our flag not only

56

represents the resiliency, courage, and pride that this country was built upon, but it also pays tribute to the brave men and women who protect our freedoms both at home and abroad. The American flag is a symbol that reminds us how we must stand together under the fifty stars and thirteen stripes to protect this nation from any threats to our democracy and way of life. Today, I encourage all to proudly display our American flag as a powerful demonstration of our citizens' basic rights to life, liberty, and the pursuit of happiness.[100]

When people look at the flag of the United States, there is an infinite number of emotions that come to bear for each of the 350 million Americans – and probably for most of the 7.5 billion people on the planet. Problems arise when we view our emotional response as the "right" one. We see someone else's reaction and then judge its "rightness" or "wrongness." Try to keep the image of the American flag in your mind as we explore another scenario which places us squarely into a world of *Ubiquitous Relativity.*

The Memorial Day Parade is a yearly tradition in Washington Township. The pageantry of all the townspeople in various uniforms transforms Main Street into a canvas of color and texture. The high school band once again resurrects John Philip Souza and Francis Scott Key. The police officers and firefighters wear starched uniforms, which stand in stark contrast to the messy work that so often defines their lives. Veterans who can walk do their best to march in step and hold their heads high. Those who cannot walk travel in slow-moving vehicles and offer waves and nods to the bystanders at the parade. Families applaud, children yell, and everywhere there are American flags.

Jack Smith is a former Army Ranger who served in Afghanistan. This day is a somber day for him. He recalls the platoon mates he lost, and the imagery of that fierce combat all comes back to him today. He had debated whether he should even come to the parade, but ultimately, he decided that those he lost would want him to be there. He is wearing his fatigues, which still smell faintly of gunpowder – an aroma that brings him right back to the combat zone. He reaches in the front pocket of his Battle Dress Uniform and finds an earplug that he used to wear when he was training on a shooting range. Meanwhile, the sounds of the sirens on the fire truck hurt his damaged ears.

As Jack watches the colors of the flag go by, he places his hand on his heart and tears up with a mixture of pride and regret. The American flag is what he wore on his shoulder into combat. To him, that cloth of stars and stripes is no less sacred than the

Bible. He is flooded with emotion as he thinks of his brothers in arms. He attempts to regain his composure and looks around at the other people near him on the parade route.

As the parade continues down Main Street, Jack stands near Rob, who is wearing shorts and a T-shirt with a picture of Disneyland. Rob appears to be texting someone, and he is typing on his phone with both thumbs while the parade passes by. He does not pick up his head except to scan the sidewalk to the left and right of him. Jack stares at Rob and shakes his head at him, thinking, "This guy has no respect for our flag. People lost lives so that he could take his family to Disneyland, and he couldn't care less." Jack contrasts his vision of the flag with his vision of Rob, and cannot believe what he is seeing. Rob, on the other hand, is in a panic. He has lost track of his son and he is texting him; he wants to make sure his son is okay and to schedule a rendezvous point after the parade. Rob happens to be a psychiatrist who specializes in helping those who have post-traumatic stress disorder.

Claire is standing on the other side of Jack and laughing with a friend. Jack looks at her, tilting his head and wrinkling his brow in disbelief. He thinks, "This woman has no respect for our flag. She is just another person excited about buying some towel for 30 percent off instead of realizing what this weekend is supposed to memorialize." In fact, Claire is laughing because she just realized that the blouse she has been wearing all day is inside out. Claire is a little slaphappy because she came to the parade straight from the airport. Claire just flew back from Normandy, France, where she was visiting the grave of her grandfather; she was there to remember him on this holiday and to commemorate the bravery he showed when he died storming Omaha Beach.

Wendy is also standing nearby. She raises her hands and yawns as the flag passes by. Jack shakes his head and looks at her with disdain. Jack thinks, "This lady has no respect for our flag. I feel bad that showing a little gratitude to those who lost their lives in service of this country is such a boring experience for her. Maybe she should just go home, lie on the couch, and watch some reality show." Wendy is tired because she was up all night preparing the street for the parade and making sure that the veterans were all assigned cars to ride in during the procession. She lost her father in Vietnam when she was very young, and has committed to helping in the Memorial Day Parade every year.

In this example, we only look at Jack and his judgments based on comparing the emotional responses he feels relative to what he witnesses from the people around him. Based on the rules in his universe, he believes that his response to the American flag is the "right" one. Jack instantly judges that the responses he sees from Rob, Claire, and Wendy show that the three of them do not have the proper admiration for the American flag. Since the responses of these bystanders are not what Jack views as the "right" ones, he decides that they are the "wrong" ones. Jack attempts to apply the rules of his universe to the universes that surround him. However, we know that each of the other people had legitimate reasons for their actions. Jack missed out on an opportunity to connect with three other people because he did not press pause on judgment.

The extra tragedy in this scenario is that Jack could have related to Rob, Claire, and Wendy and their individual experiences. Rob may have been able to help Jack with his recovery from the trauma of the war, and both Wendy and Claire, given their personal losses as a result of combat, could certainly identify with how Jack was feeling.

Instead, like humans so often do, Jack simply judges what he sees – without asking any questions or considering that he knows nothing about the other universes surrounding him at the parade. In Rob's universe, finding his son is the top priority – and this does not reduce his respect or admiration for the Stars and Stripes. Claire and Wendy both admire the American flag and have losses to show for their love of country. It just so happens that in their universes, those feelings are expressed in different ways and at different times.

Perhaps Jack missed an opportunity to ask each of these people around him what they thought of the parade. He could even have shared his own experience and emotions, given the years he was in combat. He could have asked them if they lost anyone to the ugliness of war. He would have soon found out each of their stories, and soon he would have seen his judgments were wrong and premature. This could have been the catalyst for a connection with Rob, Claire, or Wendy, or all three of them.

This is the opportunity cost we touched on earlier. Jack does not know these three people at the parade, so they are not current friends he could lose. But he loses out on the opportunity for three new connections because of his judgment and biases, which are backed up by almost no real information. All it takes is a pause in those judgments, and for Jack to ask, "What do I not know about these people I am judging?" He would soon find that the people around him at the parade are each in their own universes – and that maybe he should wait before he makes conclusions about how these people actually feel about the American flag.

CHAPTER 15

ROAD TRIP

"Language is wine upon the lips."[101]

– Virginia Woolf

In the introduction to *Ubiquitous Relativity*, we discussed how two people looking at the same wine goblet in an optical illusion could feel contrasting emotional responses. This does not come as much of a surprise. The revelation is when after looking at the same thing, one person cannot understand why the other person feels differently. This is when there is conflict between two universes, and the only way to reduce this strife is to ask questions of the other person, like "Why do you feel this way?" or "What emotion does this sense evoke in you?" In the next vignette, try to imagine a time you shared an experience with a friend and became frustrated when they had a completely different response to the experience.

Two close friends, Tanya and Nicole, are driving north up the Pacific Coast Highway in California as part of a ladies' weekend. On their left is a boundless ocean beckoning them to venture into the unknown sea, and on their right are small towns and restaurants urging them to stay on familiar ground. They are headed to a winetasting, and the vineyards they have plotted a course for are upon them now. Like many longtime friends, they think they know everything there is to know about each other. But even the deepest, most intimate friendships oftentimes only scratch the surface.

Tanya and Nicole see an old vineyard with a cobblestone main house and rows and rows of grapes in seemingly perfect symmetry. They both "checked in" on social media at the vineyard about an hour ago. Tanya has six comments under her status update from friends wishing her well, and from her husband Aaron saying, "I miss you already." Nicole has no comments on her social media page. After walking through the grounds chatting, they walk into the main building, a modern take on a French chateau. Each woman orders a glass of the same Merlot from the vineyard.

Tanya gently grabs the long thin stem of the wine glass. She can see the outline of her thumbprint. The glass feels lukewarm and it reminds her of the way the wine-glass felt at her wedding. For a moment, she thinks of her husband, and misses him – despite having only been away from his side for a short time. Tanya lets the scent of the wine flow into her nostrils before she takes a sip. She smells flowers and berries. The berries remind her of some she tasted recently while hiking through the Santa Monica Mountains with her daughter Lauren. Lauren has been doing very well at school recently, and just made the soccer team. Tanya internally beams with pride. She shakes the glass gently, because she has seen other people do that at restaurants before taking a sip. Tanya then allows herself a measured drink of the wine and swishes it around a couple of times in her mouth. She can taste the grapes now, and the alcohol smoothly flows down the back of her throat. The grapes remind her of the bag lunches her mother used to pack for her when she was going to school. Her mother is still alive, and Tanya has a moment of gratitude and feels suddenly at peace. Tanya has left her cell phone on the counter while tasting, and Nicole sees that her home screen picture is of their entire family smiling.

Nicole reaches for her glass of wine at the same time. She almost knocks the glass over, because she is wondering what her husband is doing right now. They parted on a bad note, arguing about how they were going to pay for their son John's college tuition because money has been tight. She takes note of the scent. It seems oaky, with a hint of fruit. The smell reminds her of the cabins she stayed in while at sleepaway camp. Nicole never had much fun during those weeks in the woods, because she had no friends at the camp; she was an awkward teenager and was constantly ridiculed. Her parents thought camp would help her build character and get her out of the house for a little bit over the summer. Nicole forgets that memory for a second and takes a nice swig of the wine, gulping it down quickly. She remembers getting caught drinking wine out of her parents' cellar and receiving a beating from her father.

They both put their wine glasses back on the counter. Tanya turns to Nicole. "Wasn't that delicious? I swear I could smell every grape in the whole vineyard. It is so great that we could get away like this – even though I must admit I miss Aaron and Lauren already. I'd better be careful. I don't want to get tipsy too early."

Nicole looks past Tanya and responds, "Yeah, it was okay... but nothing to write home about. I like these times away too. I wish we could do it more often."

Tanya notices Nicole has become very quiet. "Is everything okay?" she asks.

Nicole simply responds, "Yes. What are we trying next?"

Tanya is a bit annoyed, though says nothing. She gives the server a look, as if to say, "I know she is a downer, but she's still my friend." Then she pivots towards the patio en route to their car.

Tanya completely understands why the wine triggered such joy for her, but she has only a sliver of an idea why it engendered an opposite reaction in her friend Nicole. Tanya may be aware of some of Nicole's past, but since she is not living in Nicole's universe, she does not know much about the senses and emotions her friend is experiencing at this moment.

This is one very simple example of how two identical glasses of wine not only feel different physically to each woman, but also evoke strong opposite emotions in both of them. This brief moment can completely change the atmosphere on the trip. In this case, Tanya applied the standards of her universe to Nicole. If this wine she drank made her feel happy and joyous, why did Nicole not feel the same way? These moments, while brief, can strain conversations between even the best of friends and lead to long moments of uncomfortable silence.

Nicole, in turn, may see the happiness on Tanya's face and feel envy towards her. Nicole may internalize her feelings and feel that Tanya just does not care that going wine tasting is not much fun in her world – and then she might even be resentful that Tanya had pushed for this type of vacation.

In this scenario, two different universes collide. Neither is right or wrong. They are just different. An infinite amount of possible sensations stimulates infinite possibilities of emotions. But neither woman asks of each other, "Why do you feel this way?" Neither asks themselves, "Why might my friend feel this way?" Remember too that they are supposed to be best friends. Once more, we see the opportunity cost of these judgments. If Tanya or Nicole had asked the other about the reasons behind their reactions to the wine, they may have formed a deeper friendship after the wine-tasting – instead of harboring quiet resentments towards each other. Nicole could have explained her feelings to Tanya and explain why the glass of wine has left her upset. Nicole also could have shared her universe and her disdain for wine beforehand, while they were planning their vacation.

They both drank the same wine. Yet, this seemingly identical experience brought to the surface senses and emotions unique to their own universes. This is a world of *Ubiquitous Relativity*.

CHAPTER 16

HOMELESS

"Love and business and family and religion and art and patriotism are nothing but shadows of words when a man's starving."[102]

– O. Henry

As we have seen in the previous vignettes, *Ubiquitous Relativity* encompasses everyone. I am always astonished at how quickly I assess the motives and ethics of others, often after nothing more than a split-second interaction. I cheat myself of real opportunities to connect – unless I stop for a second when I see something and consider that I am only looking at things from the vantage point of my own universe.

One subject that sparks great debate and passionate opinions is the concept of a social safety net. A large group of people in the United States believes in a free market system that has winners and losers. Another bloc believes in a system that creates more equality and therefore provides support for everyone in the country. Political parties have fractured down these lines, and each election cycle, the country seems to swing in one direction or the other. Meanwhile, income inequality continues to grow, and this is a real concern for society overall.[103] Try to keep your own views on helping the less fortunate in mind as we examine another series of interactions and judgments in an everyday event.

Two men, Frank and Fred, leave their office in Midtown Manhattan. It is December and winter has begun its annual assault on exposed skin, so they are both wearing suits with long coats down past their knees. Frank and Fred walk uptown on Broadway, and they can see fine clothing and toys through the glass of each store they pass.

The two friends also see an unshaven man in filthy clothes, sitting above a subway grate. The steam coming from the tunnels below the city warms his body, but not enough to stop him from shivering. In front of him, the homeless man has an empty Styrofoam drink cup next to a cardboard sign that says "Anything Helps. God Bless You." He is repeating something incoherent – just loud enough for people to hear, yet not loud enough for them to understand.

Frank looks at the homeless man and sees the dirt on the old jacket that hangs over his shoulders. He sees the man muttering and shivering and thinks of how cold he must be on a day like today. He feels shame at the way many of our less-fortunate people have been treated. He can smell the raw body odor of the homeless man from ten feet away. He knows this scent well from all of the other people living on the streets. Frank turns away at first to avoid eye contact, but then he feels a surge of empathy. He looks at the sign again and thinks that this homeless man probably has an education but has fallen on hard times. "It is almost Christmas, after all," Frank thinks as he reaches into his pocket. He pulls out a dollar and places it into the paper cup. The homeless man mutters, "God bless you."

Fred is also looking at the homeless man and he notices the words "Anything Helps." Fred is having his own financial issues because his mother has been sick for a year now and needs help with insurance premiums. Fred has put almost every penny aside for her and has literally nothing in his pockets. He is too proud to tell Frank or anyone else at work just how strapped he is right now. He smells the body odor of the homeless man and is reminded that he has not cleaned his own clothes in weeks, because he cannot even afford to take them to the dry cleaner. He is sure others at his office are starting to notice his own lack of hygiene. He wishes he could give something, but has nothing and feels ashamed at not being able to help the homeless man. He looks down at his scuffed shoes as they pass the man on the grate.

Melissa is in a taxicab watching Frank and Fred pass the homeless man. The warmth of the heater in the taxi is a stark contrast to the cold outside, and she begins to get a little uncomfortable in her overcoat. She has just had a nice meal, and seeing the homeless man makes her feel guilty for leaving half of her lunch on the plate. She sees Frank drop a dollar in the homeless man's cup, and she watches Fred walk by without giving anything. She expected them both to give something to the man, because she sees both them in their suits and assumes they do well enough to spare a single dollar. When she sees Fred walk by without even making eye contact, Melissa shakes her head, thinking, "Typical Wall Street guy. God forbid he helps anyone else."

After walking another ten feet, Frank turns to Fred and says, "You don't have a dollar to spare for that guy? Boy, you are some kind of miser." Fred pretends he does not hear his friend, as the wind howls through the city.

This is a classic example of seeing a situation and bringing our own biases to bear without knowing anything about the other people involved or their motivations. Melissa has her own guilt about income inequality and the fact that she is able to have nice meals and leave parts uneaten. She is getting very warm and is already feeling physically uncomfortable. She clearly has opinions about people who wear suits, and while she excuses Frank because he gives something to the man on the sidewalk, she instantly judges Fred to be cheap and heartless. If Melissa had paused on judgment, she would have simply felt good about seeing Frank donate – and not let Fred's inaction get her upset.

Frank also judged Fred, by giving him a hard time about not putting any money in the homeless man's cup. But even though they are friends, he has no idea what the real situation is in Fred's life. Frank certainly could have imagined multiple explanations for Fred's inaction, and instead of shaming him based on the laws of his own universe, he probably could have guessed a few reasons why his friend did not give any money.

There are certain hot-button issues that we have to be zealous about when it comes to pausing on judgment. This is because our views are so entrenched and often so passionate that they can blind us to the truth of a situation. As we have seen in the other vignettes, there is also an opportunity cost.

In this case, the opportunity cost is the chance Frank has to form a stronger connection with Fred. Instead of making him feel guilty about not giving any money to the homeless man, he could have asked his friend if everything was okay. Fred also could have opened up his universe to Frank by sharing some of the difficulties he is going through. Either of these actions would create a new understanding between them. Perhaps Frank could help Fred with his finances or give him some ideas on how he could improve his situation.

This is why it is so important to try to ask ourselves before a judgment, "What may I not know about this situation?" If Melissa had asked herself that question, she may have paused before labeling Fred as another rich person who only cares about himself. If Frank had asked that question, he may have paused before embarrassing his friend.

CHAPTER 17

THE BRO-HUG

"And if you see me, smile and maybe give me a hug. That's important to me too."[104]

— Jim Valvano

Our universes are shaped by our experiences from birth until now. Clearly, the way we are raised as children has major implications for who we are today. Our parents and close family can disproportionately affect our emotional reactions to the world we sense around us each and every day. One of these effects is how we feel about meeting and trusting new people. Throughout the following vignette, try to imagine how you would feel about an interaction with a total stranger.

It is a typical party in Manhattan insofar as it includes a fair share of struggling artists and a fair share of Wall Street twenty-somethings still hopeful that the streets are paved with gold. The host of the gathering, Cliff, tries his best to bring a diverse crowd together for these events, but his version of varied demographics falls far short of the different cultures and people in New York City. Friends talk to each other, strangers glance at each other, and occasionally people approach unfamiliar faces. Cliff makes introductions because he likes to weave people together.

Cliff came from a lower-middle-class family in the suburbs of St. Louis, but now he resides on the Upper East Side and has made great efforts to forget his difficult youth. His best friend from childhood, Evan, has moved to New York from St. Louis recently; out of loyalty and empathy, Cliff has invited Evan to this party.

Evan lived in that same tough neighborhood just outside St. Louis. His parents were constantly fighting. His father was the domineering type who believed that a man should never cry and that there was no room for physical affection or emotion between two men. His dad was extremely homophobic and taught Evan that to be gay was to be evil. From a very young age, Evan was taught that any contact between men

– except for physical violence – was considered homosexual. He spent his entire life avoiding his father's wrath by following his every rule. Evan has never hugged another man or shared any intimate emotion with another man.

Evan is pretty uncomfortable at the party. To him, the artists do not seem to be struggling, and the Wall Street employees speak a language he barely knows. He is wearing khaki pants and a nice polo shirt, but all he sees are people who wear trendy clothes he has never seen before. He feels dressed up, but he also feels like everyone is looking at him and whispering to each other. Some are even wearing sunglasses inside the apartment. The Wall Street guys keep talking about women in the room, saying misogynistic things using terms heard on trading floors, like "I am a buyer of her." Evan has never said anything like that about any girls he knows.

Nearby, sitting among a group of men and women drinking white wine, is an artist named River. River was born in a commune in Oregon and spent most of his life there. His parents were always very affectionate with him, and he grew up with a tribe of people who always ate together and worked together for the betterment of the group. They hugged each other in the morning and at night before bed as a physical way of showing their love and connectedness. River is wearing clothes that cost hundreds of dollars and are supposed to make you look like you belong in a dive bar. His jeans are ripped in multiple places and he is wearing a concert shirt of a band that was in its prime long before he was born.

Cliff is talking with Evan and spots River a few feet away. "River, come here. I want you to meet someone," he says. "This is Evan, my friend from high school in St. Louis. He can tell you some stories about the good old days when we raised quite a bit of hell." Cliff raises his plastic Solo cup of beer to toast with his pal of many years. He then turns to his friend of few years, saying, "Evan, this is River. I met River at work. He is the head visual effects coordinator at a local post-production house in the neighborhood."

Evan thinks to himself, "What kind of a name is River? His parents had some sense of humor." He reaches out to shake River's hand. Instead, River walks past his handshake and extends both arms to hug Evan. "I am a hugger, Evan," he says.

Evan immediately recoils, grabbing River's wrists to stop him and then pulling away from the other man. "I am not a hugger," Evan says as he turns and walks away.

Cliff stands there, embarrassed for both of them after the awkward exchange. He then takes another gulp of ale from his cup. River turns to Cliff. "Your friends from St. Louis are pretty uptight."

Cliff simply shrugs his shoulders as if to say, "Evan has never been the affectionate type. What can I do about it?" Yet again, this is another example of a missed opportunity for a connection based on multiple assumptions and judgments. River assumed that because his universe encourages hugging, then all universes should as well. In Evan's universe, hugging another man is totally unacceptable. Is one universe more right than the other? River certainly thinks so, and he judges Evan to be uptight because he declined physical contact. But in Evan's universe, he was simply acting as his father taught. River goes so far as to judge all of Cliff's friends from St. Louis based on this one interaction. River could have asked Cliff if there was a reason for Evan's reticence to hug. Perhaps, given their closeness, Cliff knew Evan's family situation. Evan also assumed that a law from his universe – that it isn't appropriate to hug – applied everywhere. If Evan believed in a world of *Ubiquitous Relativity*, he may not have stormed off; he may have thought about why River was conditioned to hug strangers.

Evan could have told River he just was not big on hugging and that it was nothing personal. Note all the senses of discomfort that preceded their exchange. Evan already feels out of place because he is new to town and thinks people are making comments about the way he is dressed. It is likely that this discomfort made him even less friendly towards River before the hug than he would ordinarily have felt. The way Evan and River felt at that specific moment affected each of their judgments. Only by asking questions of each other can we even begin to scratch the surface of a universe outside of our own.

CHAPTER 18

FIRST DATE: I THOUGHT WE JUST WATCHED THE SAME MOVIE

"Well, I'm sure you'll find someone somewhere who'll have you."[105]

– J.K. Rowling

We all have different reactions to common imagery, yet we search for consensus in our reactions. We seem to constantly want validation for our opinions. One place in which I see this time and time again is in our perspectives on various works of art, from motion pictures to plays to canvas paintings.

I don't know how many times I have seen a movie I really liked, yet still felt compelled to read the critics' reviews afterwards. If I already knew I liked the movie, why did I need to confirm that others did as well? Likewise, I have attended shows and clapped at certain points simply because people around me were clapping. Was I just trying to be part of the group? Or was I afraid that if I did not applaud, it would reflect negatively on my ability to appreciate the show? I have been part of a standing ovation at the end of a musical for no other reason than because others rose to their feet before me. Similarly, I have stood immediately at the end of a play to communicate my pleasure and awe, yet still felt the need to pressure others to stand with me. Perhaps it is due to my own insecurities and lack of knowledge, but having my opinions validated is a powerful motivation to fall in line with what I view as the consensus.

As is often the case in a world of *Ubiquitous Relativity*, an issue arises when we cannot understand why someone else could see the same movie or go to the same play or look at the same painting in a museum, but disagree with our assessment of its merits. In the next vignette, we will examine this phenomenon in the context of a first date at the movie theater. We focus on this common occurrence because we tend to be especially quick to judge when we interact with potential romantic interests in a world of "love at first sight." In this vignette, try to imagine how you would feel if you and your date had completely different reactions to a movie. Would you judge them? Would you be nervous about them judging your reaction?

Many first dates in Los Angeles take place in a coffee shop or bar and last about thirty minutes. However, Abe and Evelyn, who recently connected online, have decided to go see a recently released film that Abe's friends recommended. Abe has had a tough week at work and wants to have a few laughs and not deal with anything too heavy on his Friday night. They agree to meet there, because the logistics of driving in the City of Angels require near-military planning to avoid traffic, construction, and a host of other headaches. When they meet, they exchange pleasantries and tell each other they "look better in person than online." Abe immediately notices the scent of Evelyn's perfume, because his ex-fiancée (who cheated on him three weeks before the planned wedding) wore the exact same brand.

The movie theater is on the older side, with small seats and the dull smell of popcorn permeating throughout. It appears as if the staff is on strike, because garbage is strewn over a floor still sticky from spilled soda. The air conditioning is too high, and Evelyn regrets not wearing a jacket over her tank top. The film Abe has chosen is a raucous, vulgar, and lowbrow movie about fraternity brothers going nuts on campus.

Abe is laughing pretty hard throughout the movie, but Evelyn is extremely quiet. She squirms in her seat when the humor gets more vulgar. After the credits, when the film is finished, Abe asks, "What did you think?"

Evelyn replies, "It was all right, I guess. Not really my cup of tea."

Abe looks at her with a half-hearted confused look on his face. "How could you not think that was funny?" he asked. "On your profile, it said you had a sense of humor and that was one of your strong points. I mean, that scene where everyone is getting wasted at the party – that was one of the best ever!"

After the movie, they say goodbye with an awkward handshake. Abe concludes that Evelyn isn't much fun, and he deletes her number from his phone. At no point did Abe ask Evelyn why she didn't think the movie was funny. Perhaps the cold air or the small seats in the theater contributed to Evelyn's disappointment.

If Abe had tried to learn more about the situation, he might have learned that she had a very bad experience at a fraternity house in college. Perhaps this type of film evokes fear rather than amusement for her. This could have made her resent Abe for choosing this movie and cause her to judge his character by this one selection.

Two people see the exact same movie but have completely different emotional responses. We see this time and time again, and it is what our Everlasting Equation attempts to recognize as a fact of life. The issue, of course, is when one person believes everyone should agree with their judgment of the film. Abe believes that if Evelyn does not find this movie funny, then she is unable to be fun in any situation. If Abe had asked Evelyn why she was less-than-enthused after the show, he may have forged a deeper connection than most people do on their first date. He may have come to the same conclusion about their future prospects as a couple, but he would have had much more information before making that judgment. The opportunity cost is that Abe missed out on a potential romantic or platonic connection – all because he never bothered to think about what he might not know about Evelyn's universe. Instead, as we so often do, he tried to apply the rules of his universe to someone else's universe.

In all of these situations, we can see that some of the sensations that make up the left side of our Everlasting Equation can make an uncomfortable situation even worse. The physical discomfort that Evelyn felt in the theater might have contributed to her emotional displeasure. At the same time, Abe had a tough week and the scent of the perfume triggered a memory of humiliation and shame. Evelyn could not possibly have known this without talking to him about it, but it is easy to imagine that this physical input made Abe unusually dismissive.

CHAPTER 19

SPRING BREAK

"If everything seems under control, you're not going fast enough."[106]

— Mario Andretti

Life can be full of risks and rewards. Risk tolerance varies from person to person and even over the course of a lifetime; factors including age, wealth, and genetics affect an individual's perception of risk and willingness to take risks. In the next vignette, try to think about your willingness to take risks at this point in your life.

College Spring Break in Cancún: a rite of passage and a passage of wrong. It is one of those hot mornings where the headaches spread over the students like waves washing on the sand. Some of the revelers have recollections of the night before, while some can't remember anything and some wish that they could forget the previous night. Typically, this is a time for lying on the beach and recovering, but since the sunburns are so profound (especially for the fair-skinned students from the north), a few of the vacationers decide to change the routine today.

Fraternal twins and roommates Mark and Paul and their new friend Joel decide that one way to sober up is to raise the fear factor. On a whim, they decide to leave the row of hotels that loom over the beach and go bungee jumping at an amusement park about thirty minutes away.

Mark and Paul are from an upper-middle-class family, and their parents made a lot of money in the housing and stock markets by buying some properties and shares when prices collapsed in 2009. Fortunately for them, they had enough cash in the bank to take advantage of this big opportunity. They were taught from a very young age that one must take risk in order to gain reward. When panic prevailed as asset bubbles burst, Mark and Paul saw their parents as the definition of "grace under pressure."[107]

Joel, on the other hand, grew up in a family that lived check-to-check. His father lost most of their money in the dot-com bust and never fully recovered. His mother used to tell him, "Your father takes too much risk. It finally caught up with him and now we're broke. So don't make any big plans anytime soon." From his earliest memories, Joel was taught to avoid risk completely or "wind up with the same fate as your dad."

Mark, Paul and Joel flag a taxi at their hotel. Mark says, "To the bungee jump, por favor." The air conditioning is not working, so the cab driver rolls down the windows. That lets a little fresh air in, but it is still pretty hot, and Joel can feel the sweat on the back of his legs sticking against the vinyl seats. They drive by a cross-section of enormous hotels for the tourists and shanty shacks for the locals. He feels ashamed because he identifies more with the struggling locals than the tourists flush with money to spend.

After about twenty minutes in their taxicab, they can see the large crane that will serve as the location of the bungee jump. Each of them feels the butterflies in his stomach, which mixes with a general nausea from the fiesta the night before and makes them start to feel a little queasy. Nevertheless, they exit from the taxi and start to walk over towards the line of eager danger seekers awaiting a brush with fear.

Mark and Paul are hooting and hollering, trying to psych themselves up. Mark walks up to the front of the line and then back to his friends, giving a high-five to each person he passes in the crowd. Joel has his head down and is starting to breathe heavily. People are now entering the queue behind him, so he starts to feel boxed in. He abruptly changes his mind on the whole endeavor. He turns to the twins, saying, "Guys, I can't do this. I thought I could, but I am feeling a little sick and I'm going to take a pass."

Mark looks at him with some disdain and says, "You sissy. What are you so scared of? Don't give me this nonsense about feeling sick. We are all nervous, but you have to conquer those fears. Now buck up man, you are doing this!"

Paul puts his arm around Joel and tells him, "Listen, you need to take risks in your life. Once you have landed after this bungee jump, you know how good you will feel? If you walk away, you will spend the rest of your life regretting being scared."

"Is it the money?" Mark asks Joel. "If so, I can spot you for this. It's only twenty dollars."

Joel replies, "It isn't the money, I just changed my mind. I will meet you guys back at the hotel." He then starts walking back to where the taxis congregate.

Mark looks at his brother Paul. "What a wussy," he says. "Let's lose him after this."

In this scenario, we focus on each player and their philosophies around taking risk. The brothers, Mark and Paul, have completely different attitudes than Joel, as they have grown up in very different universes. Each person senses things as part of the left side of the Everlasting Equation. Joel felt physical nausea from too much alcohol and too much sun. The sweat he felt on his legs created more discomfort, and in line for the bungee jump he felt boxed in and under more pressure. Mark and Paul didn't have the same reaction to the excesses of the night before, so they were more enthusiastic for the bungee jump. Similar inputs triggered different reactions. They all witnessed the scenery from the hotel to the amusement park. This seemingly had no effect on the twins, but for Joel it triggered shame about income inequality and specifically his own poverty. The sight of the big crane excited both Mark and Paul because they both are comfortable with risky activities. Joel had a completely different reaction due to his personal experiences with risk. In his house, risk was a four-letter curse word and he was conditioned to avoid it at all costs.

As with all the other vignettes, there are opportunity costs when people judge other universes by the laws of their own. In this story, the opportunity cost is connection between the brothers and Joel. The twins judged Joel as simply too scared of the bungee jump, and as a result they decided he was not someone they wanted to spend time with again. If they had asked why Joel didn't want to go, they might have learned more about one another. Even if Mark and Paul still believed Joel was a sissy, they may have had a better understanding of his risk aversion. Alternatively, Joel could have shared his experience instead of making up excuses for why he didn't want to take the chance of jumping off of the crane.

CONCLUSION ON THE RIGHT SIDE OF THE EVERLASTING EQUATION

This story and all the other hypothetical situations in this portion of the book focus on the right side of the Everlasting Equation. That being said, we can clearly see that both sides of our equation are constantly in play. Senses influence emotions, and those emotions then trigger judgments. Each time we add another person to an encounter, the potential for biases and prejudices expands dramatically. These situations are continuous throughout every day of our lives.

These judgments have many consequences, but some of the most frequent consequences are lost and missed connections between people. We examined the opportunity costs of these judgments in each vignette, so we can see how many connections wind up on the cutting room floor. At the same time, we can see how easy it is to pause on judgment by asking questions of people. The word "why" is usually a great first step towards understanding someone else's universe.

We may think someone is wrong because the laws of their universe do not match the laws of our universe. On many occasions, this has caused me to give up hope for connection with someone. I hear something they say or see the way they look, and then make my conclusion without the faintest idea of their motivations. This philosophy we have examined so far permeates every area of our lives, from relationships with loved ones to our interactions with total strangers.

This way of thinking has especially impacted me in the sphere of business, investing, and finance, which is where I have earned a salary for the last twenty-two years. I have been very successful at compartmentalizing my job and literally taking on a different personality at the workplace. Unsurprisingly, as I dove deeper into this new way of connecting with people, it spilled over into my life at the workplace as well. Separating my work persona from who I am at home has become increasingly difficult. I believe there are many other people in the same situation, trying to walk the tightrope between two parts of life: in the office and out of the office. In the next section of this book, we continue our journey towards a pause on judgment in the settings of the office and finance. We will look at how finance and business are two more streets on an infinite grid in a world of *Ubiquitous Relativity*.

PART 4:

Ubiquitous Relativity in Business

At the time of this writing, "America's Best First Job" is the tagline that McDonald's is using in its commercials. I happen to be one of the many Americans whose first job was at this legendary fast food chain.[108] In 1988, I was a freshman in high school and I was told it would be a good "character-builder" to start working for minimum wage (which was $3.35 per hour at that time).[109] I have spent the last twenty-two years working in finance, but when I walked into McDonald's seeking employment at age fifteen, the manager told me I was not qualified to work the register, so I began work as a cook in the grill area.

After toiling as a sub-average chef for months, I was asked by my manager if I wanted to be part of a promotional day at the Golden Arches. At this point, anything seemed better than making cheeseburgers, so I quickly accepted the opportunity. But what did I have to do? It appeared to be a simple task – all I had to do was dress up as Grimace and walk around the restaurant. Who is Grimace, you ask? He has been described in many affectionate ways, but let's go with Wikipedia's description:

> *He is a large, purple anthropomorphic being of indeterminate species with short arms and legs. He is known for his slow-witted demeanor. His most common expression is the word "duh" before every sentence.[110]*

When I put on the costume of this dubious character, I discovered it was made for a six-foot-tall person – and at the time, I was only five feet tall. The costume was all wool, with a small screen to breathe through. In the humid New Jersey summer, I was losing pounds of weight in sweat every fifteen minutes. As I stumbled, perspired, and gasped for air, I began to actually miss the grill.

My manager told me to go out to Route Forty-Six, a four-lane roadway, and wave to cars driving by. After about twenty minutes, an old Chevrolet Astro van passed by. To this day, I can still picture the scene in detail. A young boy, no more than four years of age, was looking out of the Astro's window. As the van drove by, he looked at Grimace and extended his middle finger at this lovable purple creature. What kind of a world was I living in? I quickly went back into the McDonald's, took off my costume, and quit "America's Best First Job." Any time I start to feel my ego is getting too big, I remind myself of that day in 1988. Humility in everything we do and what we think we know as "fact" is a key tenet in a world of *Ubiquitous Relativity*.

Almost everyone I know has experienced these moments when they get too arrogant and the world knocks them down a peg. The moments may not have come in the form of an encounter with a snarky child while dressed as Grimace, but they were likely just as memorable. In business, investing, and finance, there are frequent humbling moments. Because of this, business, investment, and finance are a few of the biggest tenants in a world of *Ubiquitous Relativity*. Perhaps the best way to explain is to review various aspects of our new philosophy, with a focus on finance, business, and investments.

First, people love certainty in finance (as in other areas of their lives), and often they focus on opportunities with "guaranteed" returns. Investing, however, is an inherently risky and uncertain venture – and when we look for "can't-lose" offers, we can and often do lose a lot of money.

The best way to look at both sides of the Everlasting Equation is to determine how our emotions can get the best of us and distort reality. Casinos and stock markets are great examples of this, and we will examine how both manipulate our senses and emotions.

Even with the advent of technology, most businesspeople rely on relationships to achieve and maintain success. We will see that as we expand our own universes, we dramatically increase our ability to relate to clients. It is possible to become a better employee as well as a better person. We will look at business meetings as an opportunity to consider the universe of the person on the other side of the negotiating table.

Finally, *Ubiquitous Relativity* relies on non-consensus thinking. Non-consensus thinkers change the world and profit from their willingness to challenge norms. These people, who often zig when the rest of the world zags, avoid losses by staying away from bubble-type investments that usually end very badly. It is by questioning biases and assumptions that great investors find great ideas.

As the head of an Equities Division at an investment bank in Los Angeles, I occupy many roles. I examine and suggest investments of all kinds for a variety of mutual funds, hedge funds, and other large institutions. I perform two very distinct functions. I work within my firm to specialize in how to invest, but I also have to maintain relationships with clients who each have specific objectives and goals. Therefore, in this part of the book, I will look at both the art of investing and the art of maintaining good client connections. These principles can be applied to any business that relies on relationships with customers.

I have spent most of my life compartmentalizing my behavior inside the office from my behavior outside the office – to the detriment of both. Outside of the office, I have always expressed a wide range of emotions, from joy to sadness to fear. At work, I only knew fear, and I swore up and down it was the best way to motivate people. I used to tell my employees, only half in jest, to remove all pictures of their families, because it would make it more difficult on me if I had to fire them. As a result of my appreciation of a world of *Ubiquitous Relativity*, I have begun to change my approach to management. Alas, it is a work in progress. The key theme of this section of the book is that I do not have to separate my life in the workplace from my life outside of the workplace.

I can pause on judgment in all of my waking hours, and increase connections in all aspects of my time on earth.

CHAPTER 20

THE HUMAN NEED FOR CERTAINTY IN FINANCE

"There is no such uncertainty as a sure thing."[111]

— Robert Burns

Earlier in this book, we discussed the human craving for certainty. We looked at various belief systems and their rules for living an ethical and moral life. The same desire for rules and systems exists when investors search for ways to make money. When Bernie Madoff's investments showed a small percentage return every month of every year, this was an opportunity that investors simply could not pass up. The appeal was so great that nobody bothered to even figure out how he did it. People were willing to skip due diligence, just to make sure they wouldn't miss this once-in-a-lifetime chance.

Madoff's Ponzi scheme, the biggest in history, ended in terrible pain for its investors – many of whom lost their entire life savings.[112] How in the world did the people invested with Madoff ignore the red flags that now seem obvious to everyone? In a word: certainty! The returns Madoff promised were steadier and more reliable than anything ever seen in the financial world. The certainty was uniform returns of 10 to 12 percent per year, and Madoff was able to keep the scheme going until everyone wanted their money back all at once. At that point, the only certain thing was that all of the investors' money had disappeared.[113]

Just like in life, very few things are certain in the world of investing. In life and in investing, there is generally a tradeoff between risk and reward. Generally, the more risk I take, the higher the potential reward; likewise, the less risk I take, the lower the possible reward. If I never leave my room, the risk of something negative happening to me is diminished, but I also lose the potential for positive surprises like human connections and experiences. If I travel the world, I have a lot more risk of encountering danger, but I also have a lot more potential reward in seeing new cultures and countries.

79

Almost all investing is also based on this relationship. In general, the greater the financial risk I take, the greater the potential monetary reward for me. Likewise, the less risk I take, the less upside I can expect to get from an investment. If anyone tells me there is a guaranteed certainty in the world of markets, it usually rings some alarm bells in my head. Furthermore, if someone pitches me a product that features a high return with no risk, I usually end the conversation.

As we discussed earlier in our analysis of *Ubiquitous Relativity*, the human craving for certainty leads to collisions between universes because people tend to think their belief system is the "right" one. In the investment world, this same desire for certitude can lead to huge losses.

People love to hear steadfast rules for success. In investment, many companies claim to offer a straightforward and guaranteed strategy to make money. Thousands of books offer investment rules. Not unlike the systems that we follow in other areas of life, these rules are to be followed with no deviation. The reward is simple: money! And who doesn't like money? However, in my experience working next to some of the greatest traders alive, the wizards of Wall Street are not sharing their trading advice or secret formulas for making money. They aren't getting wealthy by selling investing ideas in a computer program or a newsletter for $300 per year. The people who are spamming your email inbox with those offers are unlikely to have real solutions.

In a world of *Ubiquitous Relativity*, I must challenge my biases in order to grow. Universal rules and absolute laws collide all the time when everyone lives in their own universes. This is no different in the world of finance. When I feel sure that I'm right about an investment, I tend to discount anything that gets in the way of that certainty. When formulating an opinion, I tend to dismiss any fact that may challenge my view.

This all-too-common investment pitfall, known as sampling bias, occurs when I only look at the positive reasons of buying a stock and ignore all the potential negative outcomes. In my investing career, I have often fallen victim to this flawed way of doing research.[114] I can remember many business deals I was offered in the past. There have been many instances when business opportunities have sounded great to me. When I look back at the deals that were unsuccessful, it was often because I ignored all the parts of those deals that could go wrong.

Playing the lottery exemplifies this phenomenon. Most of the time, I buy my ticket and fantasize about all the wonderful things I will be able to do with my winnings. I rarely consider how remote the odds are of this scenario actually coming to fruition.

Another way people look at certainty is through the lens of "How much can I lose on this trade?" In this respect, people gravitate towards trades and investments where they perceive a low risk with high reward. One way this manifests itself is in the purchase of low-priced penny stocks. We have all heard and seen about the very, very few speculators who made a killing because they bought a stock for cents on the dollar and it went up 100,000 percent! But like the lottery, for every winner there are millions of losers. It looks attractive on the surface, because if I invest in a $0.55 stock, I can only lose fifty-five pennies for every share I buy. Remember, there is a reason the stock is trading for less than a dollar: it is most likely on its way to being worthless. Cheap stocks are cheap for a reason. In my investing career, I have bought low-priced stocks, hoping for a rare enormous return while ignoring that I was most likely buying a company with all kinds of issues, little to no earnings or revenue growth, and a secular decline in its business. To most people, myself included, it sounds better to own two thousand shares of a $0.50 stock than to own one share of a $1,000 stock – but in the long run, I almost always would have made more money on the one-share investment.

Is there a right way to invest? I have seen many websites offer tips on how to make money by purchasing their proprietary systems. The pitch is almost always the same: follow our instruction manual to invest and you will have success. Peddlers of investment advice often make sales because investors crave certainty in an inherently uncertain world of markets and money. There is a staggeringly large amount of media geared towards investing, including books, magazines, websites, and radio shows. The fact that there is such an abundance of guidance for achieving financial success speaks to the abundance of demand for that advice. It seems people everywhere are looking for the "right" way to invest.

I cannot count how many times I have heard advice offering guaranteed returns with no risk. It always sounds great until I reach the fine print – which usually explains that past returns are no indication of future performance. The advertisements for investing schemes are not unlike the advertisements for medications. The first few seconds discuss the benefits of the drug, and then the remainder of the pitch lists all the potential complications. On the radio, the risks are spoken in a pace many times quicker than the initial offer.

The key concept to take away from this chapter is that we should look at certainty in investing as oftentimes misguided. Pausing on judgment is a way for us to more accurately evaluate how we manage our money. If investing returns were actually more certain, there would be much less income inequality. We are apt to remember this every time we see the word "guarantee" in a sentence about investment ideas.

CHAPTER 21

THE EVERLASTING EQUATION – THE CASINO AND THE STOCK MARKET

"When the capital development of a country becomes a by-product of the activities of a casino, the job is likely to be ill-done."[115]

— John Maynard Keynes

When I think of great challenges, I think of climbing Mt. Everest, racing in an Iron-Man triathlon, and swimming the English Channel. But in my opinion, all of those amazing feats pale in comparison to the ability to walk into a casino and not play. Imagine that! You and I are walking down the Las Vegas Strip into the casino in the Caesar's Palace. We go to the center of the floor, surrounded by the lights and the sounds, and just stand there. We stand there and do nothing. We approach no tables or slot machines. We simply observe. That is one tall order! How long do you think we would be able to abstain before having to walk out of the casino altogether?

Gambling revenues worldwide continue to rise as humans continue to be drawn to games of chance at record rates.[116] The physiological and emotional reactions we experience in a casino are powerful and acutely designed to keep us coming back to gamble again and again. When we look at this phenomenon through the lens of *Ubiquitous Relativity*, we can examine what happens to us when we bet on games of chance. Investing in the stock market is different from playing table games in Las Vegas, but it can feel awfully similar. I believe that the casino is the perfect venue to observe both sides of the Everlasting Equation, because in casinos, we experience infinite combinations of sensory inputs, which stimulates infinite combinations of emotions.

When I walk into a casino, most of my senses are overloaded and overstimulated. I see slot machines of all shapes and sizes, covered in blinking lights. There are people giving each other hugs and high-fives at the craps table. I listen to the bells, the whistles, and people yelling and screaming. I hear cards passing through a Shufflemaster and then gently moving across a felt table.[117] I hear dice bouncing off the wooden rails of a craps table. The cacophony of jackpots pouring out of machines sieges my ears. I touch the five dice and select two to roll. I blow them a kiss and pray for a ricochet that lands on the right number. The chips I have in my hands are colorful and perfect circles. I stack them in tidy columns, never thinking about the fact that they represent actual money. I taste the drink that has been given to me free of charge, and I breathe easily in the oxygen-rich air. I feel alive and I feel lucky. The stimulants I observe are just a fraction of the casino features that are designed to light up our senses and our willingness to take risk – even though the odds are clearly stacked against us in almost every game. The stock market can feel eerily similar.

I do not want to give the impression that I equate investing with casino gambling (although some people swear a monkey throwing darts at a board could outperform many money managers).[118] But when we look at the Everlasting Equation, these two forms of speculation have a lot in common.

Let's look at some of the similarities between casinos and the stock market. We will hopefully realize the vital importance of recognizing all the things we do not know about our sensory inputs.

The fear of missing out is a strong emotion in a casino. Like most people, I have felt this from a young age, whether I was worrying about not being invited to a birthday party or feeling anxious over not owning a popular toy. I feel the same emotion when I walk into a casino and see other people winning all around me. I see a group of people at the craps table jumping up and down and having fun. Everyone is making money and I cannot believe I am just watching. Suddenly, I feel terrible envy because I'm missing out on all this money I could be making! All around the casino floor, I see others winning, and I cannot stand to just watch anymore. And like a bee drawn to honey, I decide I must ante up and play. The casino is counting on this.

The stock market is no different. I hear all the time about individual companies somehow having changed the world, and when I see the stock prices of these companies jump, once again I feel envy. But in a world of *Ubiquitous Relativity*, I should ask myself, "What might I not know about the senses and emotions I am feeling?" It is vital to avoid buying a stock because of fear of missing out, just as people should not play games in a casino because they see other people winning.

Over the years, I have often fallen victim to survivorship bias. This bias is the logical error of concentrating on the people or things that made it past some selection process, while overlooking those that did not (typically because of their lack of visibility). This can lead to false conclusions in several different ways. In the casino, I often focus solely on the few people I see winning – and not the multitude losing. Craps tables are not raucous and fun-loving when people are losing money. The slot machines where people are losing do not make any sounds. The people who win are always the first to tell others, and the people that have lost usually keep their underperformance to themselves. In this way, we are biased towards the survivors of the casino – "the lucky few." I often forget that for every one of those survivors, there are many more that did not survive – "the unlucky many." Casinos are designed to profit from people's inherent survivorship biases.

The same phenomenon exists in the stock market. The big-name successful money managers are always on the business networks, and their investment suggestions make it sound easy to get rich. But again, these are the survivors, and for every money manager that has great performance over an extended period of time, there are many, many more who have not survived because their performance was poor. People tend to share their successes in the stock market more often than they share their failures. It is not hard for me to tell who is making money in the stock market and who is not, because people typically don't brag about their mistakes.

What else do I not know about the situations I sense around me in the markets or in a casino? What if the person who is jumping around because they just won a thousand dollars has already lost five thousand? I may only see the celebration and assume I am missing out on something great, although usually the reality is quite different. The stock market is similar. If I bump into someone at a party, they may tell me how a stock they own just went up 25 percent – but forget to tell me that they originally bought the stock 50 percent higher. People may tell me all about the stocks they own that have gone up, without mentioning all the stocks that went down.

Again, because I have no context, I should not assume I am missing out on anything! What I see in my universe is not what is happening in someone else's universe. Whenever someone tells me about some big winning idea they had, I always ask, "Have you ever had a big losing idea?" If they answer "No," then either I have met a genuine psychic who can see the future, or I am not being told the truth.

Remember, if the winners outnumbered the losers, the casino would be out of business. The fact is that the odds are against anyone who walks on the floor. It's a fiction that the odds are in my favor, but it's still a very convincing fallacy because the inputs into my senses trigger all the emotions discussed above. The stock market – and really any kind of speculation – does not specifically advertise itself like a casino, but I have fallen prey to the very same senses and emotions multiple times. I am not judging anyone for their approach to investing or gambling, but the theory of *Ubiquitous Relativity* is critical in both these activities because they offer opportunities to pause on judgment.

The most important thing to remember is that my truth is not the truth in any situation. When I think the two are the same, I am more likely to make investments without all of the information and lose money.

CHAPTER 22

EXPANDING MY UNIVERSE TO HELP MY CLIENT RELATIONSHIPS

"The universe is a pretty big place. It's bigger than anything anyone has ever dreamed of before. So if it's just us, seems like an awful waste of space." [119]

— Contact

The main goal of the theory of *Ubiquitous Relativity* is to enhance the connections we feel to other people. I believe that the connection between a business and its customers is key to success. As the leader of an Equities Division within an investment bank, my job is to help clients make money. Our business researches stock ideas and provides them to mutual funds, pension funds, and hedge funds. If our ideas help them to increase their returns, then they will pay us for our expertise and assistance.

It may sound a little callous to say that our firm's goal is solely to make clients money, but by doing so we help people all over the world. The better a pension fund performs, the more likely it will be able to pay retirement benefits to a local police officer. If we perform well for a mutual fund, then every person who invests in those funds will do well. Parents will have greater resources to pay for their children's education, and employees who have 401K accounts will be able to retire earlier and more comfortably. For these reasons, personal connections with our clients are paramount; there is more at stake than simply money. The connection between a firm and its clients can last for decades. My appreciation of a world of *Ubiquitous Relativity* has greatly improved my relationships both in and out of the office; as I expand my own universe of experiences, I am better able to appreciate other people's universes.

The rapid pace of technological evolution has not replaced the need for customer relationships. On the contrary, as I described in the chapter about the flipside of technology, it has made it more essential to maintain spoken interactions with others. The first challenge we face in building strong relationships with our clientele is choosing the right form of communication. Today, many of us have become so used to the ease of technology that we forget the value of non-electronic interaction. Email is one of the many modes of communication we use. But as discussed earlier, when we rely solely on electronic interaction we lose the opportunity for context, voice inflection, and body language. This is why talking to a client on the phone or seeing a client in person have taken on much more value today – these forms of communication are now the exception, not the norm. This creates an opportunity for those willing to take the extra steps of connecting with clients in a non-electronic fashion.

People respond to the voice of another person. More often than not, clients appreciate when a businessperson is willing to connect with them on a different level. When I think about the electronic communication I receive on a daily basis, I can't help but yearn for the days when phone calls and office visits were commonplace. (Perhaps I am becoming an old curmudgeon after all.) Robo-calls and mass e-mails with all kinds of offers and solicitations seem to be more popular now than ever before.

Each day, a client may receive thousands of these e-mails but only a handful of calls with a live person on the other end of the phone. One business may solicit new customers solely by instant messages, and another may go visit its prospective clients. I have found that customers generally respond to the effort of non-electronic connection.

It is very likely that the customers of any business have wide and varied interests and come from all different demographics. In a world of *Ubiquitous Relativity*, each of our customers lives in their own universe. Therefore, each of our customers senses the world differently and has different emotions related to those senses. All of our customers are unique. This should not be earthshattering. But if we have hundreds of customers who all live in their own universes, how can we be the most effective business? The more interests and experiences we have, the more customers we can relate to on a personal level.

Millions of people interact with many customers every single day. Businesses of every type, from hardware stores to restaurants to apparel retailers, service hundreds or even thousands of people daily. The more a company knows about its customers, the better it will be at servicing their needs.

Even though a thousand different customers may buy the same toy from a toy store, each different customer has their own unique set of interests. Imagine you are the owner of that toy store and are deciding who to hire or who to promote. Who is more likely to connect with the most clients?

- Someone who has played with all of the toys, or someone who has tried only a handful of them?
- Someone who is multi-lingual, or someone who only speaks one language?
- Someone who has travelled to the manufacturing location to see how the toys are made, or someone who has never left the town where the toy store is located?
- Someone who has been to competitors' stores and seen how they do business, or someone who has no idea about the sales methods of other toy stores?

This list of questions can continue indefinitely; the more expansive an employee's universe, the more clients they can relate with. The better the relationships between the employees and the customers, the more likely it is that the business will succeed.

The other challenge, once we have established the way we communicate, is always to ask questions of our customers so that we can learn about their universes. To continue with the toy store scenario, consider all the questions an employee could ask a customer:

- How old are your children?
- Are you aware of the most popular toys right now?
- Have you ever shopped here before?
- Do you need help locating anything?
- Are you local or from out of town?
- How has your day been?
- Is the gift for a birthday?
- Is your child a boy or girl?

Again, there are infinite questions one could ask a customer. The key takeaway is that the more questions employees ask, the more they will learn about the customer's universe. Because each universe is unique, each customer has to be treated as a person unto himself or herself – not simply as "the customer."

There is a saying in most businesses that "the customer is always right." In a world of *Ubiquitous Relativity*, it is critical to understand why that specific customer is right. When it comes to each customer's universe, what do we know (or just as importantly, what do we not know) that could make us more effective in servicing the customer's needs? If strengthening the human connection is our goal, then strengthening the interpersonal bonds between businesses and customers is part of this aim.

CHAPTER 23

NON-CONSENSUS THINKING

"It's better to walk alone than with a crowd going in the wrong direction."[120]

— Diane Grant

The theory of *Ubiquitous Relativity* is a non-consensus idea; it requires people to question their prevailing views, which are typically formed through their societal norms. If people look at some of the greatest entrepreneurs and investors, they see a common thread: non-consensus ideas. One of the most frequent events in history is the appearance of "bubbles" and their subsequent bursts. From Dutch tulips to the dot-com boom to the housing bubble, we see the power of crowd behavior. The people who profit the most from these situations are those who act early enough to buy the asset before the boom and sell before the asset bubble bursts. To accomplish this, these people have to think differently than most. I missed my chance to get out of some of my investments before the bubbles burst, because I did not see what should have been obvious. Two examples where I wish I had practiced non-consensus thinking stand out in my memory.

In 2000, we were in the midst of the great Internet bubble, and I was a twenty-six-year-old trader working at J.P. Morgan. To help build our presence in Europe, management asked me to fly overseas and meet accounts in Italy, France, and England. The purpose of the trip was to convince the managers of these accounts to give more business to J.P. Morgan. Before I went to the airport, I picked up my itinerary from our executive assistant in charge of logistics for the firm. I was to fly Virgin Upper Class and stay in five-star hotels. The assistant also handed me a very thick envelope.

"What is this?" I asked.

"Oh, that is your spending cash. It is one thousand dollars in Lira, one thousand dollars in Francs and one thousand dollars in Pounds." So there I was, a twenty-six-year-old walking into J.F.K. Airport with money in every pocket I had. I could barely close my jacket. I thought this kind of lifestyle would go on forever. Spoiler Alert: it didn't.

At no point during the dot-com boom did I ask, "Does it make sense that a young kid is traveling like a millionaire on the company dime? What could go wrong?" I never considered that I was part of a horde of investors all doing the same thing. I did not sell my internet stock investments because I thought the ride would never end. Therefore, like many others, I made and then lost a lot of money because I could not see the forest through the trees.

Several years later, in 2007, I completely missed the housing bubble that was building in the United States. I remember my brother, God bless his heart, sitting on a couch in my family room. He had just left the Army and was telling me about a guaranteed way to make money: house-flipping. "It's really easy, Ian," he said. "You just buy these condos in Florida. You don't even have to put any money down. Then you sell them in a month at a profit."

I asked him, "What if there isn't a buyer?" Spoiler Alert #2: he didn't have an answer for me. Here was another period in our history where the horde of investors and speculators piled into an asset class (in this case, homes) and drove the prices to unsustainable levels – eventually leading to a crash. I was one of the many who owned a house at the time, watched it go up in value, and did not sell it when I should have. There were people who made a lot of money by buying houses before the bubble built and selling houses before the burst. But these people were non-consensus thinkers. They went against the crowd. I did not, and I saw the value of my house go down precipitously. My mortgage payments became too much for me to bear and I was sinking further in debt every day. I just barely managed to sell my house short and avoid foreclosure.

Large swaths of the business world function the same way. If too many people jump on a boat at the same time, it could sink. One of the biggest downfalls of consensus thinking in business is when a company suffers from groupthink. Groupthink, a term coined by social psychologist Irving Janis in 1972, occurs when a group makes bad decisions because group pressures have deteriorated judgment. Groups affected by groupthink ignore alternatives and tend to take irrational actions that dehumanize other groups. A group is especially vulnerable to groupthink when its members are similar in background, when the group is insulated from outside opinions, and when there are no clear rules for decision-making.[121] I have been in organizations that have suffered mightily because they fell victim to groupthink.

Non-consensus thinking is a defense against groupthink, and it's absolutely necessary in a world of *Ubiquitous Relativity*. We are products of our societies, and we develop views similar to those around us. Therefore, our "crowd" tends to have consensus views. Ancient scientists and philosophers theorized that the earth was flat for thousands of years.[122] This remained the prevailing view, even as evidence began to build to the contrary. Those who argued the earth was spherical were ridiculed, until explorers proved that the world was in fact round. There are plenty of other ideas that were non-consensus at the time that went on to change the lives of everyone on the planet.

In 1876, Alexander Graham Bell became the first inventor to be granted a patent for the telephone. Bell tried to sell his invention to Western Union and they didn't accept his proposal because of the "obvious limitations of his device, which is hardly more than a toy." Instead, Bell formed his own eponymous company. Ten years later, over 150,000 people owned telephones.[123]

In 1899, *The Literary Digest* magazine wrote about the new concept of an automobile, saying, "The ordinary 'horseless carriage' is at present a luxury for the wealthy; and although its price will probably fall in the future, it will never, of course, come into as common use as the bicycle." Henry Ford went on to design the Model T in 1908, and the rest is history.[124]

Imagine having to go back to the days when people had to do their Christmas shopping on the street. Not a pretty thought, is it? In 1966, *Time* magazine interviewed people about the future of technology. Some predicted that even if remote shopping turned out to be feasible, it would end up being a complete failure. Jeff Bezos challenged that consensus view, and Amazon.com is now one of the largest companies in the world.[125]

These are just a few of the many notable examples in history when someone challenged conventional wisdom – and by doing so, changed the world. The theory of *Ubiquitous Relativity* is totally dependent on this type of thinking. We may hear things about other cultures or civilizations from the people we live with, but how can we ever really know what is true unless we question our assumptions, biases, and judgments? If we sit around our family dinner tables and hear consensus views about groups of people, we can either accept what we are told or go out and find out for ourselves.

The only way to determine consensus is to talk to others and learn more about other universes. If we do not learn about other universes, then we substantially limit our ability to understand the truth. The great thinkers over the course of humanity's arc of existence questioned the consensus views of the time and took great risks in doing so. We don't have to circumnavigate the globe or invent the telephone to show we are non-consensus thinkers. To show the same kind of bravery, all we need to do is question any existing view that is consensus in our universe. It is always risky to challenge the prevailing views, but in a world of *Ubiquitous Relativity*, the increased human connections are worth those risks.

CONCLUSION TO UBIQUITOUS RELATIVITY IN BUSINESS

I used to think of my ability to segregate areas of my life into compartments as an asset. I could spend ten hours of my day in an office, acting as if I were devoid of emotion and impervious to any views other than my own. I always believed that my employees needed to accept my way of leadership or face termination. In essence, my truth, as it related to the way I took charge of an organization, was *the* truth.

The second I walked out of the office, I would try to form peer-to-peer relationships. I thought I was very good at leaving all of my poor relationship skills at work. I was certain I was a different person in social settings away from my daily corporate setting. I couldn't understand why I had such a difficult time connecting with people outside of the office as well.

Through my exploration of a world of *Ubiquitous Relativity*, I have realized that not only is it impossible to compartmentalize areas of my life, but it is both unhealthy and detrimental to my existence as a whole. Almost all of my leadership failures – and there are many – can be traced to my desire to impose my will and the laws of my universe on everyone around me and everyone who reported to me. Now, with a clearer head, I can see that my platonic and romantic personal relationships outside of the office often failed for the same reason.

Over the last few years, as this new way of looking at the world has shifted my views, I have realized that who I am at work and who I am at home are one and the same. If I am to truly make a difference in this world, I need to be willing to connect with everyone – not just certain people in certain types of relationships. I now view total strangers as potential connections, whereas before I had no interest in getting to know anyone outside of a close inner circle of people I trusted.

Almost everything I do in the business and investing world has changed as a result of this new way of thinking. I look at investing and leadership differently. I accept that there is almost no certainty in finance and I consider every investment I make through the relationship between risk and reward. I am sensitive to how my senses and emotions engender biases that are detrimental to succeeding in business. I make an effort to expand my universe further so that I can relate to more clients and more colleagues. I ask more questions of people who report to me, so that I can become a better boss. Most importantly, I try to challenge consensus views. I no longer accept ideas as fact simply because they are believed by the majority. I question all of my own assumptions about my prejudices and biases.

In business as in all areas of my life, I now do my best to pause on judgment. These changes in my approach have led to a much more rewarding work experience and demonstrate to me that the areas of finance, business, and investing all reside in a larger world of *Ubiquitous Relativity*.

PART 5:

Exercises to Appreciate Ubiquitous Relativity

Hopefully, at this point in the book we have a much better idea of the many variables in the Everlasting Equation. We should also appreciate just how difficult it is to pause on judgment. In many cases, pausing on judgment does not come easily. When we do this, we begin to question our own assumptions – which can become quite uncomfortable. Therefore, we must practice; with each repetition, the discomfort diminishes. Because many of our judgments are often a product of our fears, by working on a pause in judgment we are also working on a pause in fear. When we confront these fears, we may see our lives change. Not unlike conquering a fear of heights or dogs, we can put a dent in our fears of other universes.

Like any goal in life, there are typically multiple ways to achieve this. The methods I employ are by no means the only ones or the right ones for everyone. In fact, they may be precisely the wrong practices for some individuals. There are infinite ways to work towards acknowledgement of a world of *Ubiquitous Relativity*. Like the different universes espoused in our philosophy itself, each person will have a unique approach. We can start by not judging someone else's process at improvement as better or worse than ours. Remember, if no two universes are alike, then we cannot possibly know what the best way is for anyone else to reach their goal of pausing on judgment. For this reason, I speak in the first person in all of these exercises.

I will detail a few of the practices that have worked for me during my attempts at a psychic change. The practices are continuous and dynamic because there is no finish line. I am certain I will not wake up one morning and be free of all judgment. My goal is simply to pause in my judgments, even if only for a moment.

The eternal question for many of us seems to be: How do I live a good life? It seems every day there is a new self-help book, new diet, and new spiritual program billed as the answer. I believe that they might all work, yet I also believe that perhaps none of them will work. I know that I have no idea what will work for someone else. This is why my philosophy of *Ubiquitous Relativity* is a contradiction in and of itself. I believe in its power because it changed my life, but I cannot assure anyone reading this book or talking with me that it will work for them. In this spirit, I can only discuss my own program.

I will discuss five different practices I employ to help me appreciate a world of *Ubiquitous Relativity*. I call them Perception Minute, Unique Universe Tally, The Symbiotic Universe, Universe Ownership, and Comfort Zone Departure. A common theme through all of these exercises is I constantly ask myself, "What do I not know about this person or situation?" Usually, the answer is almost everything – but each of the practices I use has slightly different nuances to arrive at that answer and work on different areas of my mind and body.

Each exercise is different, but the goal throughout is to pause on judgment. I try to pause on judgment because I realize that my universe is unique and unlike any others. The more I learn about other people and their universes, the more likely I am to connect deeply with my fellow humans.

CHAPTER 24

PERCEPTION MINUTE

"If the doors of perception were cleansed every thing would appear to man as it is, Infinite. For man has closed himself up, till he sees all things thro' narrow chinks of his cavern."[126]

– William Blake

Many great athletes prepare for games by spending hours envisioning themselves making the big play over and over again. Hockey players may imagine various scenarios on the ice or picture themselves firing a puck into the back of the net. Placekickers in the National Football League may imagine the entire process, from the snap of the football to its placement by the holder to the kick to the ball that sends it sailing through the uprights – so when the game-winning moment does occur, they feel like it has already happened. Likewise, most performers mentally rehearse the motions and lines of a play or a musical before the curtains go up on the actual show.

I try to approach the situations throughout my day in the same manner. As part of a meditation each morning, I think about the previous day and recall a situation that filled me with judgment. Maybe it was when a man cut in front of me in line at the movie theater. I think of what my initial judgment was in that situation: perhaps fear, anger, jealousy, or any of the many emotions we have discussed throughout this book. I ask myself, "What did I not know when I made that judgment? When that person cut in line at the movie theater, what could have been the reason? Is it possible he was rushing to save a place for a handicapped child? Could he have been visually impaired and was rushing to get a seat near the front of the theater? Could his movie have already started?" In almost every situation, there are questions like these that I could ask myself. Although I cannot go back in time and change the judgment I made in the moment, I can think about that situation so if it occurs again there might be a pause in my thought process. If I can recall a scenario from yesterday and reimagine it with a positive ending that pauses on judgment, then if a similar situation presents itself today, I may be ready with a better response than I had yesterday.

I can certainly think of many recent encounters where I made a judgment despite knowing almost nothing about the situation. Using the example above of the man who cuts in front of me in the line for the movies, how did I respond? Did I pause before the judgment? If not, how could I have responded differently? As part of the Perception Minute, I will take a situation like the one at the movie theater and either think about the good reaction that I had or reimagine the situation with a better reaction than I showed. Again, the goal is that the next time someone cuts in front of me in line at the movies (or another similar situation), I will have already rehearsed this event in my mind and I am prepared to respond in a less judgmental fashion.

I always find driving to be one of the most stressful activities, especially in Los Angeles. So let's look at a few different scenarios I have experienced in my car and consider how I might pause in judgment the next time I encounter them.

Situation #1: I was driving in my car yesterday and a man cut me off without signaling. I felt fear and anger.

Was there a pause in judgment? No. I immediately swore at the driver and sped up to tailgate him to signal my anger. I then pulled up next to him to give him what I refer to as the "New Jersey Stare."

How would I like to have responded? I could have paused for a second and asked a few questions: Why is he in such a rush? Could he be late to an important job interview? What might be going on his universe that he felt it necessary to drive aggressively? Could he just have found out some really bad news from his wife and is speeding home to see her? Is it possible he simply did not see me?

Perception Minute: I will imagine a scenario where a similar thing happens on the road, but I respond differently. I may be scared for my safety – but before I swear, tailgate the man, or give him a death look, I ask myself a few questions about his universe.

Situation #2: I am driving behind a car on a side road. On the back of the car, there is a bumper sticker that supports a politician I dislike. I become angry at the thought that the person driving the car has the same values as the politician. I speed up and look for an opportunity to beep my horn at the driver.

Was there a pause in judgment? No. The bumper sticker immediately raised my ire and I generalized all people that support that politician as having the exact same views.

How would I like to have responded? I could have paused for a second and asked a few questions: How do I know the person driving the car is also the owner of the vehicle? Could the person have a legitimate reason to support that candidate? Is it possible the driver does not support that politician anymore and has not bothered to remove the bumper sticker?

Perception Minute: I will imagine a scenario where I am behind another driver with a bumper sticker I disagree with based on the beliefs in my universe. I will think about seeing the same bumper sticker, but before judging the driver as an enemy and looking to express my displeasure, I will ask myself a few questions about his universe.

Situation #3: I have been sitting in traffic for 30 minutes, waiting to get off an exit. While I am sitting there, a woman driving a car speeds up the shoulder, bypassing most of the traffic. I swear at her as she drives by and hope she gets pulled over by the police.

Was there a pause in judgment? No. Even though she was doing something illegal and unsafe, I assumed there was no possible justification for her driving this way. I was scared and I felt it unfair that I had to sit in traffic while she did not. My first reaction was to swear at her and wish she were pulled over by the police.

How would I like to have responded? I may have paused before concluding this person was a jerk and decided not to let her actions dictate my judgments of her. I may have thought, "Why is this driver in such a hurry? Maybe she has something really important to get to quickly? Is it true that I have no idea what that is?" Even if I knew the reason the driver was flying past traffic illegally, and in my universe the reason was "wrong," that does not mean the reason was not of utmost importance to her.

Perception Minute: I will imagine a scenario where I have been sitting in traffic and a driver attempts to bypass the entire line by driving on the shoulder. I will visualize the driver trying to then cut in front of me. Before rejecting the person outright by judging her on this action alone, I will consider there may be reasons unbeknownst to me that she needs to bypass this traffic.

Situation #4: I am driving on the highway and there is a woman in the next lane driving a new Ferrari. I immediately conclude that she has a great life, is rich, and is wildly successful. I feel worse about my own life because my car does not compare well to the Ferrari.

Was there a pause in judgment? No. I assumed that because a person is driving a really nice car that her life is perfect and she is successful. I could have realized how little I know about this person next to me. Was the car hers? If I don't know this person at all, how can I declare her life a success? What if other areas of her life have fallen apart and she is driving this car to escape it all? The numbers of things I do not know are infinite!

How would I like to have responded? I would not assume anything about her life solely based on material goods. Likewise, if others do not possess many material items, I will not assume their lives are unsuccessful. Next time, I will focus on my life and not compare and contrast with other lives based on external sensory inputs in my unique universe.

Perception Minute: I will imagine different material items and see them for what they are: material things. I will not make any assumptions on the people attached to those cars, clothes, and houses. If I see someone in a Ferrari, before I render any judgments I will remember that there are an infinite number of things I do not know about the situation.

After experiencing any of the situations described above, most of us move on and do not spend much time thinking about it. This logically begs the question: If we will forget about these encounters in short order, why do we expend so much energy on our judgments in the moment? If we see these situations in our mind before they happen, but with a pause in judgment this time, the hope is we will successfully pause in judgment in the next similar situation. We have the opportunity to avoid a collision with another universe.

CHAPTER 25

UNIQUE UNIVERSE TALLY

"To be yourself in a world that is constantly trying to make you something else is the greatest accomplishment."[127]

– Ralph Waldo Emerson

Every biology student accepts that each person has his or her own unique genetic code. Likewise, crime scene investigators believe, without a shadow of a doubt, that each person on the planet has their own unique set of fingerprints. Beyond that, it is quite easy to forget just how unique each of us is among the global population of 7.5 billion people. That is why one of the exercises I like to do once a week is a Unique Universe Tally.

There are three questions I try to answer to sum up my uniqueness:

1 What is my unique quality?

2 How unique is it?

3 Why am I grateful for this quality?

I think it is incredibly important to remind myself of all the blessings I possess in this life, instead of what I do not have, most often as it relates to superficial material goods. Through a Unique Universe Tally, I can see my own distinctive qualities and appreciate the unique qualities of others. It is also a great way to see how I fit in the world – and how the world fits me. Each quality can be researched reasonably accurately so that I can learn about my special traits. Once I understand the various probabilities of certain characteristics, then I can see the incredibly low odds of living in the same universe as someone else.

I typically pick five of my traits. I use a search engine to research the odds of possessing this specific quality. It is not easy to find precise odds of having a single

100

trait. But, I have found that I can get a pretty close approximation from searching for the uniqueness of one of my qualities through a simple search on the internet. In the example below, I want to know the odds that another person on Earth has these same qualities. In other words, how unique am I? For this exercise, I chose five of my qualities:

1 I speak English.

2 I suffer from tinnitus.

3 I have been in an airplane.

4 I have 20/20 vision.

5 I am not right-handed.

The next step is to examine each of these qualities individually for their uniqueness. Then I spend some time thinking about why I am grateful for this quality.

Quality #1: I speak English.

How Unique Is It? 1.5 billion, or 20 percent, of people worldwide speak English.[128]

Why Am I Grateful? I can communicate with almost everyone around me and if I need help they will understand me.

Quality #2: I suffer from tinnitus.

How Unique Is It? Several surveys made around the world have found that when asked, around 5 percent of all adults say that they experience tinnitus in one or both ears.[129]

Why Am I Grateful? Even though my hearing has been damaged, I am still able to converse and form connections with others. I also have the means to stay up-to-date on this condition and, if there ever is a cure, I may have the resources to find it.

Quality #3: I have flown in an airplane.

How Unique Is It? Fewer than 18 percent of people alive today have flown.[130]

Why Am I Grateful? I have the means to fly on an airplane, and I'm able to travel to many more places in the world. As a result, I have met people who speak a different language than I do. I have connected with people who live in completely different cultures than I do. I have met people who have never been to America, so I have had the pleasure of sharing my culture with others.

Quality #4: I have 20/20 vision.

How Unique Is It? Only about 35 percent of all adults have 20/20 vision without glasses, contact lenses, or corrective surgery.[131]

Why Am I Grateful? Because I have 20/20 vision, I am able to see the world perfectly without the need for any assistance. Every moment I get to see the beauty all around me in nature. I can also avoid danger because I can see clearly.

Quality #5: I am not right-handed.

How Unique Is It? About 90 percent of people are right-handed.[132]

Why Am I Grateful? Because I am left-handed, I am able to do certain tasks in ways that many others cannot. Most importantly, I have both of my hands and I am in great healthy condition.

Each trait may not seem particularly special on its own, but when I take a look at the probability of all these qualities appearing in one person, I can start to see the uniqueness of my universe.

I put these five different traits into a Uniqueness Formula:

(Odds of Quality #1) X (Odds of quality #2) X (Odds of quality #3) X (Odds of Quality #4) X (Odds of quality #5) = Odds of a person having these 5 qualities

So using the examples described above, the odds of a person speaking English are 20%, the odds of suffering from tinnitus are 5%, the odds of having flown in a plane are 18%, the odds of having 20/20 vision are 35%, and the odds of not being right-handed are 10%.

I plug these odds into the Uniqueness Formula:

(20%) X (5%) X (18%) X (35%) X (10%) = 0.0063%

I then multiply this incredibly small percentage by the overall population of the world. The result is that out of a population of 7.5 billion, there are only about 472,000 people in the entire world who speak English, suffer from tinnitus, have flown in a plane, have 20/20 vision, and are not right-handed.

Remember these are only five different qualities! With each additional trait that we add to the formula, we begin to recognize the depth of our uniqueness. We do not need to know genetic code or have a fingerprint database to see how our universe is unlike any other.

This exercise reminds me of my individuality. Additionally, it reminds me that everyone around me is incredibly unique. I can identify some attributes of each person I come into contact with, but they have infinitely more traits that I do not know about. As we multiply the odds of having these traits in the Uniqueness Formula, we see that each of us truly does look and act like we are in our own universes.

I gain a lot by going through this exercise. I take a few moments each week to learn about my universe. By learning about the probabilities of a few of my characteristics, I appreciate my own uniqueness. This exercise also gives me gratitude for who I am instead of focusing on who I am not. When I complete a Unique Universe Tally each week and see my own individuality, I can also imagine how other people's universes are also unique. I find further evidence of a world of *Ubiquitous Relativity,* because when I look at a person I may see the color of his or her eyes – but have no insight into any of the other traits below the surface.

CHAPTER 26

THE SYMBIOTIC UNIVERSE

"Judge a man by his questions rather than by his answers."[133]

— Pierre-Marc-Gaston de Levis

I can usually look in the rearview mirror of my life and understand the sources of my thoughts and actions. Because each person exists in a separate but parallel life path, I have a very difficult time appreciating what is in everyone else's rearview mirrors. I find asking people personal questions helps me to overcome this. Even the most basic of inquiries can help me get a deeper look into another person's universe.

One of my most everyday forms of interaction is when I introduce myself to someone. But how often am I the person initiating this interaction? The truth is that for most of my life I avoided new connections. I was that person who could walk by the only other person on a beach for miles — and not even lift my head to say hello or smile. I now challenge myself to improve my connections with others, through an exercise I call The Symbiotic Universe.

When I meet someone for the first time, I usually shake hands and try to remember that person's name (a challenge in its own right). Very often, I see certain people almost every day and never stop to introduce myself. There are people I work with, who I see every day — and even after years on the same job, I still do not know their names. I see the same people in the dog park on Saturday mornings, and still they remain nameless. I do not have a good reason for avoiding these basic human interactions. I know that once I get to know someone's name, I feel more connected to them. Going forward, when I see someone I recognize, I will do my best to introduce myself.

The only way I am able to learn about others after my initial impression of them is to initiate a conversation. I see this as an opportunity to learn something I do not know about that person. This sounds a lot easier than it is, because I am forced to be present and actually listen and learn. This is difficult, considering modern technology makes it easy to disappear into social media and other electronic worlds. I often find the mundane to occupy moments of discomfort or silence.

It is no easy task to break free of my natural tendency to avoid the discomfort of a conversation with someone else. I often struggle to find the words to even attempt to connect with someone else. The actual number of questions I could ask of a friend or stranger is limitless and each question could trigger a host of interesting answers. What is most important is that I am willing to ask questions of others, so I get a glimpse into their universes. I am embarrassed to admit how much time I have spent talking about the weather because I was too absorbed in myself to pursue any deeper connection.

I have a simple technique to make sure I ask people about themselves. I like to think of a "question of the month" to ask every person I come into contact with, from good friends to total strangers who wait tables or work at the register of a department store. I try to make it more specific than the clichéd "How you doing?" Instead, I can ask a similar question in a way that helps me to learn something. For instance, I may ask, "What was the best part of your day?" This is a question that requires some thought and helps me to identify with people. Perhaps someone replies that the best part of their day was a story they heard on public radio, or that is was surfing during the sunrise. I may have listened to the same radio broadcast or have surfed the same waves, and therefore we may have a shared experience.

When I meet a couple for the first time, one of the things I try to do is ask them, "How did you meet?" I learn quite a bit about their story and how I can relate to it. It is also fun to watch a couple answer this question, because it usually brings out happiness and nostalgia – and oftentimes a very funny story.

The key to making a connection is to listen to the answer to any question I choose to ask. It does not help make a connection if I ask someone a specific question and then move on to something else before they answer. I try to look in people's eyes during conversation because it helps me to connect more with them. I also try to have my phone put away during this interaction. I know that I personally feel terrible when someone asks me a question but then starts scrolling through their phone before I am finished answering.

As difficult as it is for me to ask specific questions of someone, it is even more challenging to learn what those answers really mean to that person. One of the ways I go deeper in connecting with someone after they may answer my question is simply to ask "Why?" In a theoretical situation, a female co-worker may be wearing a yellow shirt. If I ask, "Is yellow your favorite color?" I may get a response that indeed it is. Perhaps she says no and then tells me her dearest color is purple. If I continue by asking, "Why?" I can only imagine all the new things I can learn about her universe via that simple question.

Beyond the basic question "Why?" I try to also ask specific questions about shared experiences. This helps me understand how my universe is different than someone else's universe. Imagine another possible situation: I am walking on the beach with my brother. I may ask, "What do you see in that sunset?" I can always follow up with "Why?" The description of any visual sense offers a glimpse into another person's world. There are infinite possible answers I may hear, and each could enable me to understand a little more about my own brother. Imagine if he describes an old house on the hill where we used to live, and tells me the sunset reminds him of eating dinner outside with everyone. He remembers the conversations we used to have and all the laughter. Someday, he would like to do the same thing with his family, and he is saving money to buy his own house where he can see the sunset. Perhaps I had previously judged him as being cheap or not taking enough vacations. With this one question, I learn that my judgments were misguided and now I understand more about why he is the way he is with money.

I also have an opportunity for connection if I go out to dinner with a friend. I may ask, "Have you ever had this kind of food before?" If the answer is yes, I can ask, "Where?" "When?" or "Did you like it?" If the answer is no, I may ask, "Do you like it?" or "Would you have it again?" Who knows what I may learn, but it is safe to say I will hear something I did not know about my friend. I may learn about a vacation where they had this food and they may tell me about some unique life-changing experience from that trip. I may rethink a judgment I had about them as I gain knowledge about their universe.

In another potential connection, I may be walking through an indoor food market with a new girlfriend. The smells of various foods are everywhere and the aroma of the baked goods section is particularly potent. I may comment on the smell of the pies and cookies coming from the ovens. I can turn to her and ask, "What does that smell remind you of?" When she answers, I can follow up with "Why?" or "Was that a good time in your life?" I have the possibility of connecting on a deeper level with my new girlfriend by learning more about her universe. Depending on the memories that scent triggers for her, I will consider how baked goods may or may not fit into our life. If the memory is a bad one for her, it is possible that she feels a bit unsettled once the smell enters her nose. If we come across a similar situation, I will be less likely to judge her change in mood, because I will understand that in her universe, that sense is processed differently than in mine.

If I accept the premise that I know little to nothing about the other universes around me, then it is safe to say that others around me know very little about my universe. For the same reasons that I judge others, others will judge me. In many ways, it could be an added benefit and an opportunity to share some of the details of my universe with others.

There are many ways to give people a glimpse into my world, but the one with the most opportunities to practice is my answer to the question, "How are you?" No matter how well I knew the person asking that question, I have rarely answered with anything other than "Good" or "Okay." Sometimes I responded this way out of habit, but oftentimes it was because I was not prepared to share my true feelings; instead I opted for a generic coat of armor.

What if in response to being asked "How you doing?" I answered honestly – whether my response was good, bad, or indifferent. Am I more or less likely to have a sincere conversation with someone? Now imagine the scenario in reverse. I ask people how they are doing, and they respond emphatically with any answer instead of the generic "Good." Am I more or less likely to engage people and ask why?

I sense things I have in common with people all the time. I have the ability to form a connection by remarking on the common thread that I have with others. If I see someone wearing an Army hat, I can easily start a conversation with them based on my experiences at West Point. If I see someone wearing a hockey jersey, it is not difficult to initiate a discussion about ice hockey, given it was a sport I played my entire life.

In essence, when I see others, I have a choice to start a conversation with them. If I learn about experiences our universes both possess, I can reach out and try to form a connection. If I say nothing, then there is the opportunity cost of a potential relationship.

Each of us has experiences unique to ourselves, but we also have experiences that are similar to those of the people around us. There are times where these shared experiences can be the key for getting through trauma. One of the reasons why Alcoholics Anonymous works is because it brings people who share an experience together. There are help groups for recovery from all kinds of difficult events. Most are based on a group of individuals who are able to move forward in life by sharing their trauma. These support networks succeed because the participants are willing to share their universes with each other.

Other clubs that facilitate connection are oftentimes formed by each member's willingness to discuss the traits of his or her universe. Book clubs bring together people of all different kinds of universes to discuss the meaning and lessons of a piece of literature. Each person connects to one another because the participants are willing to share about their own experiences. In this way, what each participant finds unique can turn out to be a common thread and a new connection.

The Symbiotic Universe is an exercise designed to encourage a mutually beneficial relationship between different people. I challenge myself both to question others and to share with others. Through this process, I give myself a much better chance of turning a total stranger into someone I can connect with on a higher level.

CHAPTER 27

UNIVERSE OWNERSHIP

"Attack the evil that is within yourself, rather than attacking the evil that is in others."[134]

— Confucius

One of the key goals in a world of *Ubiquitous Relativity* is to pause on judgments. A great way to pause on a judgment is to acknowledge the inherent biases in my own universe. I have the ability to turn inward before I make a conclusion, simply by asking, "How do the judgments in my universe play a part in this situation?" This is probably the most important question that I rarely ask myself, but I work at pausing on judgments and turning inwards through an exercise I call Universe Ownership.

I rarely ask this question because it requires me to take ownership of my words and actions — instead of shifting all the blame and responsibility to others. Imagine how different any disagreement or argument could be if all the parties involved asked themselves this probing question. This process is quite a chore for me, because it is so much easier to point fingers. Many of the times that I disagreed with people over the course of my life, I focused on what the other person did (or did not do) to upset me. Asking this question means that I have to take some of the blame — and I don't know about you, but this has never been my first instinct.

In the Universe Ownership exercise, I think about something that is bothering me or a grudge I have against someone, and I question my own role in the matter. The goal of this exercise is to turn inward and examine my own universe before I criticize the other universes I touch every day. In each thought or situation, I should be able to ask five different questions about my own universe and about why I might be responsible for some part of the conflict with others.

I list some different examples below — but the most important takeaway is that I

109

am partially responsible for creating the situation I resent. In each instance, I describe a potential negative feeling I might have and then I list different questions I could ask myself to determine my universe's role in this situation. These questions are only a small sample of all the different ways I can examine my own universe before judging the universes around me. The exercise can be done spontaneously or on a set schedule. All I need to do is identify an issue I am experiencing and then write down five questions I could ask to aid in accountability.

Let's start with everyone's favorite topic: the workplace. For the sake of analysis, let's assume that I am miserable at work. Spoiler Alert: this applies at least some of the time! At these moments, I go into the "poor me" mindset and think of all the ways work is a drag on my life. I run through the usual reel of complaints. My job stinks, but I need a paycheck. I get no emotional satisfaction from what I do for a living because I do nothing for society. It really is a shame because I will be one of those people who wasted their lives in an office. Instead of moping around the office, I may decide to probe the role of my universe in these thoughts, by asking any of the following questions:

1 Why am I not getting any emotional satisfaction from my job?

2 Am I challenging myself each day to learn something new?

3 Am I building emotionally rewarding relationships with my co-workers?

4 Have I really thought about how my job contributes to society as a whole?

5 Are there people I don't know who may benefit from the job I do?

These are a handful of the infinite questions I could ponder about my role in this resentment. Each question helps me pause on judgment and really think about how I play a part in my own misery.

Let's look at another one of people's happiest subjects: their parents. The relationship between children and their parents is complex, so I will focus on a hypothetical scenario where every time I visit my parents, I seem to have the same negative experiences engendered by the same interactions. On the drive home, I seem to always conclude that the cause of the animosity is that my parents just don't get it and never will understand me. They treat me like a child even though I am a grown adult. Every time I call my father, he reminds me of how all his friends have grandchildren and that I am way behind the curve. My mother always assumes I need money. The easy way for me to reconcile with my parents' words and actions is to lay all the blame at their feet. The more difficult way is to examine how my own universe contributes to these feelings towards my parents. I could ask some tough questions of myself to establish my role in this unrewarding relationship:

1 Why do they treat me like a child?

2 Why does my mother assume that I need money from her?

3 Have I asked them why they treat me this way?

4 Do they view me as a child or is this only my imagination?

5 How long has this been happening?

Once again, if I ask these questions I may pause on my judgment of Dad and Mom. By owning my universe, I am taking responsibility for my actions that contributed to the issues I am having with my parents.

I have had my share of good and bad dating experiences. Perhaps this is one universal truth! On the dates that went badly, I was always lightning-fast to cast stones (figuratively, of course) at the girl across the table in the coffee shop. Without fail, I concluded that I was charming and thoughtful and that I could not possibly be the one responsible for things not going as hoped. I would say things like, "This girl was so boring. She took almost no interest in what I was saying and was yawning throughout the meal. I could not wait until the date was over." Anyone who knows me would agree about the ridiculousness of that analysis. Instead, I might take my universe to task by asking:

1 What questions did I ask on this date?

2 Did I really want to know more about her, or did I assume she was boring because she did not talk about herself?

3 Did I dominate the conversation and give her no chance to open up about things that interest her?

4 Is this a common thread throughout my dating life?

5 Is it possible she thought I was boring and tuned out as a result?

I do not have kids, but if I did I am sure the following scenario would happen plenty of times: my children won't listen to anything I say to them. I try to discipline them properly, but no matter what I do, I cannot get them to follow through on any directives I give them. I feel confident that the source of the tension is the children. As I analyze the reasons I am not getting the response I desire from my kids, I look at my own universe and ask:

1 How have I treated the kids so that they are acting this way?

2 Have I been communicating my thoughts well with the children?

3 Does my wife have the same perception?

4   Have I asked my children if there is an issue with our communication?

5   Have I sought the advice of others to see how they have successfully communicated with their kids?

Relationships between children and parents are some of the most complicated and difficult. When I ask myself where my responsibility lies as the parent, I may be able to improve connections with my children.

Clearly, there are infinite statements and situations like the ones mentioned above. The goal of each specific situation or resentment is to ask myself, "What is my role in this?" I do this exercise because my objective is to pause on judgment and appreciate how my universe is unique. The more I can determine how my judgments are an issue in my interactions with others, the more likely I am to succeed in forming true bonds.

I inevitably realize that no matter how lopsided the fault seems, I do in fact play a role. Learning what this role is and being intellectually honest enough to check my actions will help to make my universe stronger and help me gain further respect for the universes of others.

CHAPTER 28

COMFORT ZONE DEPARTURE

"We can easily forgive a child who is afraid of the dark; the real tragedy of life is when men are afraid of the light."

– Proverb

I have preached time and time again, to anyone who would listen, that one of the keys to a rich life is getting out of one's comfort zone. But as is often the case, I talked the talk but did not walk the walk. I would tell mentees and friends that a little discomfort is a good thing because it means your experiences are growing and your connections are increasing – but when I looked at my own life, at times I found myself on what seemed like a circular treadmill. I did many of the same things at the same time each week, rarely making an effort to break that schedule. During my journey into a world of *Ubiquitous Relativity*, I soon realized that one of the keys to pausing on judgment is experiencing those things that I have been judging without even trying. This is why I now do an exercise I call Comfort Zone Departure.

It makes logical sense that the more diverse a universe, the more likely it is to share some qualities with other universes. Within my universe, I live in a comfort zone that encompasses the things I know the best and most of my core beliefs. This comfort zone applies to various aspects of life. For instance, I usually eat only a narrow selection of foods, watch only a few television shows, read from a handful of book genres, and regularly spend time with a specific group of people.

Two of the main tenets of a world of *Ubiquitous Relativity* are that I live in my own universe and that I know very little about the other universes. It would serve me well to experience different, unfamiliar, and uncomfortable things. This way I expand my known universe and can better identify and respect other universes I come into contact with each day.

113

Sometimes when I talk to people about leaving my comfort zone, I get the sense they expect me to do something dangerous like jump out of a plane or go on some adventure around the globe alone. That may be necessary for a small minority of people, but most of us have very small comfort zones. We may not realize it, but even very slight changes in our daily activities can cause great initial discomfort.

For me, leaving my comfort zone can involve doing something as simple as changing the route I drive to work or the radio station I listen to during the drive. I may leave my comfort zone simply by trying a new kind of food for the first time or walking around a neighborhood I have never been to before.

The rewards of this exercise are truly astonishing and span the entire spectrum of life. As we discussed earlier, from a business perspective, the more customers I can relate to, the more there is to talk about – which helps me to build a relationship and increase sales. The more I can share memories of a similar experience, whether on a first date or during a brief discussion with someone I just met, the more relationships can be formed. The other benefit of leaving my comfort zone is that I am less likely to judge someone simply because of something that is unfamiliar to me. For example, maybe I find out that someone is a vegan. I may have preconceived notions of what living with this kind of diet means about a person. If I have never eaten at a vegan restaurant, how would I have any idea what vegan food actually tastes like or even what is on the menu? If I were willing to leave my comfort zone and try a vegan dinner, perhaps I would be less likely to judge the person. This is not to say I have to like the food, but at least there would be some common ground before I made my decision about this other person whom I know very little about.

I know when I have left my comfort zone – because simply put, I feel uncomfortable. This discomfort manifests itself in stress, fear, or any number of other emotions. But like any new thing, once it becomes more familiar, those physiological reactions decrease in frequency and intensity. The first time I go to a new city, I always feel out of place and lost. The city seems very large and I do not know the landmarks, the restaurants, or how to get around. With each day in the new environment, I get a little more comfortable because I learn and experience new things. Eventually, a city that initially felt extremely uncomfortable to me becomes familiar.

We can do the Comfort Zone Departure exercise as often as we like. The first step is to set specific goals for a certain period of time. I like to use one month as a time period because that gives me enough time to plan an event outside of my comfort zone. I typically start by thinking about a specific interest of mine. I think about my comfort zone for that interest, and then I think about my discomfort zone related to that interest. I then can come up with an action plan to leave my comfort zone and try something new to expand my universe.

This is how a template for this exercise might look:

Interest: Food.

My Comfort Zone: American, seafood, Italian.

My Discomfort Zone: Indian, Thai.

Goal: I will try Indian food this month.

Action: Make reservations at an Indian restaurant.

These action steps to leave my comfort zone do not have to be done alone. It is great to enlist others in these activities because it can make the new experience more enjoyable for everyone.

Another example, based on my interest in the arts:

Interest: Stage arts.

My Comfort Zone: Plays, musicals.

My Discomfort Zone: Opera, classical music.

Goal: I will attend an opera this month.

Action: Buy a ticket for the opera.

By no means do I need to restrict myself to just one action to leave my comfort zone each month. People can set as many different goals as they like, but it is important to make sure it is achievable. Planning just a few actions means that there is a better likelihood of completing the tasks.

Interest: Reading.

My Comfort Zone: Fiction by American or British authors.

My Discomfort Zone: Poetry, non-fiction.

Goal: I will read a non-fiction book this month.

Action: I will borrow or buy a non-fiction book.

There is also no guarantee that leaving the comfort zone will result in a new source of contentment. I may try a new kind of food and decide that one time was enough. But how will I ever know if I do not try new things? I can see that by trying new things, my known universe rapidly expands. As I touched on earlier, this applies to daily routines as well. If I look at my daily schedule, I can cherry-pick different activities I seem to do repetitively.

Interest: Cable news.

My Comfort Zone: More liberal networks.

My Discomfort Zone: More conservative networks.

Goal: I will watch a conservative news network each night for one week.

Action: I know which news networks tilt conservative. I will watch the nightly show on that network at the time I normally watch the news program on the channel within my comfort zone.

If I can keep an open mind as I venture outside of my comfort zone, it helps me to live in a world of *Ubiquitous Relativity*. The ultimate goals here are to connect with other people and to pause on judgment. It requires practice to go from comfort to discomfort in the actions I take and the judgments I make. The Comfort Zone Departure exercise requires me to make a habit out of living with the discomfort. I literally schedule my own discomfort in order to ultimately become more comfortable with the world at large.

CONCLUSION TO EXERCISES TO APPRECIATE UBIQUITOUS RELATIVITY

"Champions keep playing until they get it right."[135]

– Billie Jean King

I have found that I don't just naturally get better at pausing on my judgments – instead, I have to truly work at pausing on them. The five exercises outlined in this part of the book – Perception Minute, Unique Universe Tally, The Symbiotic Universe, Universe Ownership, and Comfort Zone Departure – are part of what I do to appreciate a world of *Ubiquitous Relativity*. However, these are only the exercises that work for me right now. I cannot stress enough that they may not work for everyone, and there may even come a time when they do not work for me either.

It took me a lot of time to find the best ways to practice pausing on my judgments. One thing was certain: no matter what method I used to try to improve my appreciation of this new philosophy, each exercise only worked with a lot of practice. There are reasons why it is hard to keep New Year's resolutions or to become a virtuoso. It takes a lot of hard work. This is no different – it is quite a challenge to reconfigure one's mind and biases. The good news is that we do not need to be virtuosos in a world of *Ubiquitous Relativity*. We only need to strive to be a little bit less judgmental than we were the day before. I have no illusions that I have come anywhere close to applying this philosophy perfectly throughout my daily routine. I simply hope that today I may pause on a judgment for one split second more than I did yesterday. If I can do this, I consider myself wildly successful.

CONCLUSION TO UBIQUITOUS RELATIVITY

"All men are created equal."[136]

– Thomas Jefferson

In a world of *Ubiquitous Relativity*, we suggest a slight but significant change to Thomas Jefferson's legendary proclamation; we declare that "all universes are created equal." Jefferson assumes that we are all "created equal" and that "equal" is a universal and all-encompassing term. I do not know if we are "created equal," but I am confident that the way people interpret the word "equality" is as different as people themselves.

Instead, if we agree that only the universes people live in are equal, we take away the infinite number of measurements we use to compare people. If I believe that all universes are created equal, then even if I am six feet and two inches tall with a 180 IQ and three billion dollars in my bank account, these characteristics are irrelevant when I compare myself to others. If those traits matter, they only matter in my universe. In someone else's universe, totally different metrics may matter.

The *Oxford Dictionary* defines "equal" in its adjective form as "being the same in quantity, size, degree, or value," in its noun form as "a person or thing considered to be the same as another in status or quality," and in its verb form as to "be the same as in number or amount." If we look at each of those word forms, we can see some issues. As an adjective, what does it mean for people to be the same in size, degree, or value? Who defines the value of a person? As a noun, how does one describe the status or quality of a person? Each person has their own concept of what it means to be a quality human being. I am not trying to pick on every word, but simply to show that a term like "equal" invites all kinds of judgments based on each person's definition.

Some may say this is simply a case of semantics, but I firmly believe that there is a big difference between comparing one person to another person and comparing one universe of existence to a different universe of existence. That is the key ethos in a world of *Ubiquitous Relativity*. We want to pause on judgment, and the best way to start that process is to fight our basic instinct to make comparisons between ourselves and others. I frequently hear people ask questions like "How do I compare to him? How do you think I measure up to her? Where would you put me on a scale relative to him or her?" These questions beg for judgments and invite prejudices.

117

In a world of *Ubiquitous Relativity*, it seems to me that the answer is, "You do not compare to him or measure up to her. You are each in your own universe. Whatever comparison you are inviting me to make is irrelevant, as your metrics only apply to your universe and my metrics only apply to mine."

There are also the moments where people tell each other, "I know how you feel," or "I have been there too." There is nothing wrong with relating to others and showing empathy to our fellow people. In fact, that is one of our goals with *Ubiquitous Relativity*. But how can anyone truly know how another person feels? If both you and I lost our fathers to cancer, does that mean we know how one another feels? In a world of *Ubiquitous Relativity*, all we truly know is how we feel in our own universes. I do not know all the senses you felt when you lost your father or all your unique experiences that triggered your response to those senses. All I can do is ask what you sensed and how you felt. I may relate to some of those senses and emotions, but I will never be able to say with certainty, "I have been there too."

Living in a world of *Ubiquitous Relativity* is not easy. It is a world that challenges some of our basic instincts. This is simply because we ask questions of others – and we ask questions of ourselves. We always hear about what "society" would think of our decisions. I am not sure who decides what "society" actually means, but it seems it all comes down to what each individual person thinks it means. Nevertheless, we each have a concept of how we are supposed to live, and this concept involves quantitative milestones we need to reach to be successful. Often, we look at our own lives relative to the lives of others, as if we were employers comparing resumes of people who want to work in a particular company. When evaluating our lives and the lives of others, do we focus on things like where we went to college, our annual income, our house, our car, or our children's accomplishments? I know that I have used many of these measuring sticks to determine if someone is "successful" or "unsuccessful." All this time, I never considered two pertinent points:

1   Why are these the questions I ask to compare myself to others?

2   Why do I assume others use these same yardsticks?

A world where we pause on judgments seems about as instinctual as running into a burning building. But like the brave firefighters who do this, we too can be brave in our lives. Firefighters retrain their minds to overcome fear of a known danger. One can only overcome this fear through practice, dedication, and preparation. I believe it is just as difficult – and equally as heroic – to question one's assumptions about the world and overcome the fear of new experiences and of new ideas that are wholly foreign and unfamiliar.

Our Everlasting Equation tries to frame how we truly live in our own universes and how little we know about the other universes we come into contact with each and every day. It shows how our different physiologies shape how differently we each sense the world. Just as importantly, our emotional responses to these senses create judgments, which are often made quickly and without any information. We have discussed multiple examples of how our judgments warp our views and lead us to misguided conclusions.

A new and scary reality as I write this book is "fake news." Stories are created and distributed to coerce people to believe things that are not true. We read news headlines and make broad conclusions before knowing any other information. If we live in a world of *Ubiquitous Relativity* and stop to ask questions, could fake news have the same impact? Imagine if a fraction of the billions of people who use social media and get bombarded with real and fake information stopped for one moment to wonder why they were seeing each story. People may ask themselves, "Why am I seeing this purported news? Is it possible that it's not true? What is the author trying to accomplish?"

On the flipside, *Ubiquitous Relativity* is not an end point with people cheering at the finish line. Instead, it is the sound of the wind and birds chirping during a hike through the woods – during a hike that is unique to each person. There are moments when I am climbing the hill and times when I am cruising down it. The key is to look at the person on the trail next to me and simply accept that I don't know anything about their hike. This is hard work and it is a daily practice. This means that I have to really want to pause on judgment in order to improve. The methods I use to progress in a world of *Ubiquitous Relativity* are merely ways that work for me, and I am sure there are an infinite amount of other ways to pause on judgment. It doesn't matter to me how we come to appreciate *Ubiquitous Relativity*. It doesn't matter to me what people call it. All I pray for each day is to have the strength to admit that my world is not *the* world.

Because I spent half my life in finance, I know that *Ubiquitous Relativity* has definite practical applications for business. I cannot remember how many meetings and negotiations I participated in where all I thought about was what I hoped to achieve by its conclusion. In hindsight, if I had thought about what the person on the other side of the negotiating table wanted to achieve, I would probably have been more successful in attaining my own desired outcome. I rarely thought, "What does this person or company want and why do they want it?"

The positive results of living in a world of *Ubiquitous Relativity* are endless. Two of the root causes of conflict around the world are our judgments towards others and our biases in favor of our own beliefs. When people speak, look, or worship differently than we do, we frequently perceive them as alien and to be feared. Imagine if, for a split second, we paused on those judgments. What if we asked that person with a different set of beliefs, "Why do you have that ethos?" Could we avoid bloody conflict if we simply asked each other "Why?" I have no illusion of stopping all wars, but if we could stop one battle by asking each other a simple question, wouldn't that be a great start?

The journey I am on in this world of *Ubiquitous Relativity* continues to unfold. Each day, I am more convinced that my truth is not the truth. But what is "the truth"? The closest I can come to defining the truth is to frame it as the sum of as many individual truths as possible. The more people contribute their experiences and connect with each other, the closer we get to the truth. Likewise, what is outer space other than the sum of each individual universe?

My belief in *Ubiquitous Relativity* challenges and changes my universe daily. A little while ago, my wife and I met a woman on the beach with her two children. I am not sure how the topic came up, but she mentioned that her children were homeschooled. In my head, I had concluded that these kids were in trouble because they would not know "reality." I judged that the woman was making a terrible mistake. And then another thought came into my mind: I have only learned a bit about homeschooling over the course of my life and cannot remember a single person I knew who actually learned in a non-traditional environment. I stopped my judgment in its tracks and remember telling my mind to shut up and acknowledge that I know nothing about this woman's universe. I have a moment or two like that every day now. It's a start.

I do not know the solution for how to live the "right" life. I could not chart a path to Enlightenment. I do not know how to define "spirituality." I also have no expectation that I'll ever be able to answer those questions. There is something about a connection with another person that helps me accept the fact that I don't have the answers. All I know is that my life feels better when I am tethered to others. The person I meet for the first time, the good friend I get to know more intimately, or the wife I get to fall further in love with all make my universe larger and more rewarding.

There are 86,400 seconds in a day. I have a choice with each of the judgments I make for many of these seconds to either accept them or challenge them. Imagine if each of us on the planet took one or two of those 86,400 seconds each day to question one of our judgments. We could change the world.

EPILOGUE

I eventually spoke to both of my parents about six months after completing this book. After much consternation, I decided to tell them both "my truth." From the perspective of someone who was hoping for fireworks or a Hollywood ending to this story, it was anti-climactic. I chose to meet each of them alone in successive days at the same diner in New Jersey. My message to both of them was brief and direct. I told them that I remembered the abuse from when I was younger and, even though it had not really ever been discussed, I carry it with me every day. I continued to tell them that this conversation we were having was not about getting them to apologize or extracting the figurative pound of flesh. I simply wanted to unburden myself of this weight I carried from the abuse and tell them that I in fact remember.

My mom cried and apologized. My dad seemed sad and regretful, but detached. That was it. I talked to each of them for about an hour and they discussed their memories and their mistakes. We went on a few different tangents and I did my best to keep them on topic.

After each meeting, I got back on the train into New York City. I thought for a while about each conversation. I was at times sad and at times relieved. But most of all, I was in acceptance. I accepted the one certainty that has echoed around my head for years now: Each person lives in their own universe, and that included my parents.

I left something at the diner after the discussions with each of my parents. When I walked through the glass doors, out into the open air, I left the expectation that somehow they would remember the events of my childhood the way I recalled them. I didn't only unburden myself of "my truth." I also let go of any hope of "their truth" mirroring "my truth". I no longer felt like I was fighting for retribution at every turn. I stopped trying to either justify or condemn their behavior. I simply said what I needed to say to let that chip on my shoulder break off and realized that I can dictate the terms of these relationships.

Currently, I talk to my parents occasionally and see them once or twice a year. It is always civil and at times we have nice conversations. Am I free of the trauma of the abuse? No. Do certain situations still make me uncomfortable? Yes. I have done work around that reality for years past and will continue to do so for many years to come. I don't, however, spend any time looking for the "Why" of the abuse anymore because I live in a different universe than each of my parents. Instead, I spend that headspace thinking about ways I can be a better person by pausing on my own judgments. That is *Ubiquitous Relativity*.

NOTES

[1] "Utopia." The word was first used in the book *Utopia* by Sir Thomas More in 1516. It is an imagined place or condition in which everything is perfect.

[2] *Stress in America: The State of Our Nation*, American Psychological Association, published November 1, 2017, https://www.apa.org/news/press/releases/stress/2017/state-nation.pdf.

[3] Robert Frost, "The Road not Taken," in *Mountain Interval*, (New York: Henry Holt and Company, 1916), 9.

[4] "Water Lilies" A series of approximately 250 oil paintings by French Impressionist Claude Monet (1840–1926). The state of France built a pair of oval rooms at the Musée de l'Orangerie as a permanent home for eight water lily murals by Monet. I witnessed them in person in April 2017.

[5] Brian Greene, *The Fabric of the Cosmos: Space, Time and The Texture of Reality*, (New York: Vintage Books, 2005), 133-134.

[6] *Merriam-Webster*, s.v. "ubiquity (n.)", accessed December 2016, https://www.merriam-webster.com/dictionary/ubiquity.

[7] *Merriam-Webster*, s.v. "relativity (n.)", accessed December 2016, https://www.merriam-webster.com/dictionary/relativity.

[8] Worldometers, accessed December, 2016, http://www.worldometers.info.

[9] John Keats, "Ode on a Grecian Urn," 1820.

[10] The quote has been attributed to a seminar that Jung attended in Zurich on March 25, 1931. It's reported in the following book:
C. G. Jung, *Visions: notes of the seminar given in 1930-1934*, edited by Claire Douglas (Princeton: Princeton University Press, 1997).

[11] John 8:32, "Then you will know the truth, and the truth will set you free," *The Bible*: New International Version, accessed January 2017, https://www.biblegateway.com.

[12] Ralph Waldo Emerson, "Experience" in *Essays: Second Series*, (Boston: James Munroe, 1844), found on American Transcendentalism Web, http://transcendentalism-legacy.tamu.edu/authors/emerson/essays/experience.html.

[13] Francis Bacon, *The Advancement of Learning*, originally published 1605, (New York: Project Gutenburg, 2014), https://www.gutenberg.org/files/5500/5500-h/5500-h.htm.

[14] Although it is often argued that knowledge of the theorem predates Pythagorus (570 B.C. – 490 B.C.), the theorem is named after the Greek mathematician.
Wikipedia, s.v. "Ancient Greece," last modified February 13, 2018, 18:51, https://en.wikipedia.org/wiki/Ancient_Greece.

[15] "The Pythagorean Theorem," Math Planet, accessed January 2017, https://www.mathplanet.com/education/pre-algebra/right-triangles-and-algebra/the-pythagorean-theorem.

[16] The Ten Commandments are first revealed in Exodus, and repeated in Deuteronomy.
Exodus 20:2-17, *The Bible*: The Old Testament, Bible Info, accessed March 2017, http://www.bibleinfo.com/en/topics/ten-commandments.

[17] The Five Pillars of Islam are the five religious duties expected of every Muslim. The five pillars are mentioned individually throughout the Quran and are listed together in the Hadith when he was asked to define Islam.
"Five Pillars of Islam," Religion Facts, accessed February 2017, http://www.religion-facts.com/five-pillars-islam.

[18] Norma Milanovich and Shirley D. McCune, *The Light Shall Set You Free*, (Kalispell: Athena Publishing 1996), Part 2.

[19] *Merriam-Webster*, s.v., "universal (adj.)" accessed December 2016, https://www.merriam-webster.com/dictionary/universal.

[20] *Merriam-Webster*, s.v., "law (n.)" accessed December 2016, https://www.merriam-webster.com/dictionary/law.

[21] "What is Theravada Buddhism?" Access to Insight, accessed February 2017, https://www.accesstoinsight.org/theravada.html.

[22] Matthew 7:12, *The Bible*, King James Version.

[23] Dr. Tony Alessandra, "The Platinum Rule," *Alessandra*, accessed March 2017, http://www.alessandra.com/abouttony/aboutpr.asp.

[24] "Meta-Ethics," Philosophy Index, accessed March 2017, http://www.philosophy-index.com/ethics/meta-ethics/.

[25] "Plato," Biography, accessed March 2018, https://www.biography.com/people/plato-9442588.

[26] John Locke, *Second Treatise of Government*, (1690; Project Gutenberg, 2010), https://www.gutenberg.org/files/7370/7370-h/7370-h.htm.

[27] John Locke, *An Essay Concerning Humane Understanding*, (London: 1689), http://www.earlymoderntexts.com/assets/pdfs/locke1690book1.pdf.

[28] Wikipedia, s.v. "Groundwork of the Metaphysics of Morals," last modified December 4, 2017, 13:53, https://en.wikipedia.org/wiki/Groundwork_of_the_Metaphysic_of_Morals.

[29] "Universal Declaration of Human Rights," United Nations, December 10, 1948, http://www.un.org/en/universal-declaration-human-rights/.

[30] Ayn Rand, *Atlas Shrugged*, (New York: Random House, 1957), Appendix.

[31] William Shakespeare, *Hamlet*, edited by Barbara A. Mowat and Paul Werstine, (New York: Simon & Schuster, 2012), 3.1.108.

[32] The source of this quotation is the subject of debate, but it has been attributed to Albert Einstein.

"It Has Become Appallingly Obvious That Our Technology Has Exceeded Our Humanity," Quote Investigator, accessed March 2017 https://quoteinvestigator. com/2012/10/25/tech-exceeded/.

[33] Dr. James McPherson, "A Defining Time in Our Nation's History," *Civil War Trust*, accessed March, 2017, https://www.civilwar.org/learn/articles/brief-overview-american-civil-war.

[34] "Global Health Observatory (GHO) data," World Health Organization, accessed March, 2017, http://www.who.int/gho/mortality_burden_disease/life_tables/situation_trends/en/.

[35] Twitter and Facebook Terminology.

[36] World Emoji Day, accessed March 2017, http://worldemojiday.com.

[37] "George Carlin Quotable Quotes," Goodreads, accessed March 2017, https://www.goodreads. com/quotes/7926-meow-means-woof-in-cat.

[38] All translations from "Google Translate." Accessed March 2017.

[39] Genesis 11:9, *The Holy Bible*, accessed April 2017, http://biblehub.com/genesis.

[40] Kim Ann Zimmerman, "Declarative Memory: Definitions & Examples," *Live Science*, February 5, 2014, accessed March 2017, https://www.livescience.com/43153-declarative-memory. html.

[41] Benjamin Whorf, *Language, Thought and Reality*, (Cambridge: Technology Press of Massachusetts Institute of Technology, 1956), 147.

[42] Stephen R. Anderson, "How many languages are there in the world?" *Linguistic Society of America*, accessed April 2017, https://www.linguisticsociety.org/content/how-many-languages-are-there-world.

[43] Matthew 6:22-23. In the Bible, Matthew reveals, "The eye is the lamp of the body. If your eyes are healthy, your whole body will be full of light. But if your eyes are unhealthy, your whole body will be full of darkness. If then the light within you is darkness, how great is that darkness!"
  Living With Faith, "The Generous Eye," accessed March 2017, http://www.living-withfaith.org/blog/the-generous-eye.

[44] "What is 20/20 Vision?" University of Iowa Hospitals & Clinics, accessed May 2017, https://uihc.org/health-library/what-2020-vision.

[45] "Difference Between Near and Far Sighted," Fort Lauderdale Eye Institute, accessed July 2017, www.flei.com/blog/difference-between-near-and-farsighted/.

[46] Alexandra Ossola, "The World is Rapidly Becoming More Nearsighted," Popular Science, February 18, 2016, http://www.popsci.com/nearly-5-billion-people-will-be-nearsighted-by-2050.

[47] "Farsightedness," National Eye Institute, accessed May 2017, https://www.nei.nih.gov/sites/default/files/health-pdfs/Farsightedness.

[48] "Facts About Color Blindness," National Eye Institute, accessed May 2017, https://nei.nih. gov/health/color_blindness/facts_about.

[49] "Ishihara's Test for Colour Deficiency: 38 Plates Edition," Colblindor, accessed May 2017, http://www.color-blindness.com/ishiharas-test-for-colour-deficiency-38-plates-edition/.

[50] "Astigmatism," Healthline, accessed May 2017, http://www.healthline.com/health/astigmatism#overview1.

[51] "Astigmatism," Eye Health Web, accessed May 2017, http://www.eyehealthweb.com/astigmatism/.

[52] Dave Rothstein, "Do we see the same stars from above and below the equator?" Cornell Education, last modified December 10, 2015, http://curious.astro.cornell.edu/about-us/120-observational-astronomy/stargazing/how-the-motion-of-the-earth-affects-our-view/732-do-we-see-the-same-stars-from-above-and-below-the-equator-beginner.

[53] Wikipedia, s.v. "If a tree falls in a forest (George Berkeley)," last modified February 1, 2018, 03:17, https://en.wikipedia.org/wiki/If_a_tree_falls_in_a_forest.

[54] "Hearing Tests," Patient, accessed May 2017, https://patient.info/doctor/hearing-tests-pro.

[55] "Summary health statistics for U.S. adults: National Health Interview Survey," 2012, U.S. Department of Health and Human Services Centers for Disease Control and Prevention, National Center for Health Statistics, (Hyattsville: DHHS Publication, February 2014), https://www.cdc.gov/nchs/data/series/sr_10/sr10_260.pdf.

[56] Howard J. Hoffman, MA; Robert A. Dobie, MD; Katalin G. Losonczy, MA, et al, "Declining Prevalence of Hearing Loss in Us Adults Aged 20 to 69 Years," *JAMA*, March 2017, https://jamanetwork.com/journals/jamaotolaryngology/article-abstract/2592954.

[57] "Quick Statistics About Hearing," National Institute on Deafness and Other Communication Disorders, accessed June 2017, https://www.nidcd.nih.gov/health/statistics/quick-statistics-hearing.

[58] "Understanding Tinnitus Basics," WebMD, accessed June 2017, http://www.webmd.com/a-to-z-guides/understanding-tinnitus-basics.

[59] "Aging changes in the senses," Medline Plus, accessed June 2017, https://medlineplus.gov/ency/article/004013.htm.

[60] "Your ears differ," Hear It, accessed June 2017, http://www.hear-it.org/Your-ears-differ-.

[61] "Why Everyone Hears the Same Sounds Differently," Knowledge Nuts, March 31, 2016, accessed June 2017, http://knowledgenuts.com/2016/03/31/why-everyone-hears-the-same-sounds-differently/.

[62] "Vertigo," WebMD, accessed June 2017, http://www.webmd.com/brain/vertigo-symptoms-causes-treatment#1.

[63] Robert W. Rand, "How many people have vestibular disorders?" *Rand Acoustics*, accessed June 2017, http://randacoustics.com/how-many-people-have-vestibular-disorders/.

[64] From *Madame Bovary* by Gustave Flaubert, originally published 1856. Retrieved from: "Gustave Flaubert Quotable Quote," Goodreads, accessed July 2017, https://www.goodreads.com/quotes/46318-never-touch-your-idols-the-gilding-will-stick-to-your.

[65] Carolyn Gregoire, "How Our Sense of Touch Affects Everything We Do," *Huffington Post*, January 20, 2015, accessed July 2017, http://www.huffingtonpost.com/2015/01/20/neuroscience-touch_n_6489050.html.

[66] Hazel Thornstein, "Names of Tactile Disorders," *Livestrong*, June 13, 2017, accessed July 2017, http://www.livestrong.com/article/172305-names-of-tactile-disorders/.

[67] Ibid.

[68] "Understanding Psoriasis—the Basics," WebMD, accessed July 2017, https://www.webmd.com/skin-problems-and-treatments/psoriasis/understanding-psoriasis-basics#1.

[69] "Psoriasis," American Academy of Dermatology, accessed July 2017, www.aad.org/media/stats/conditions/psoriasis.

[70] J. D. Salinger, *The Catcher in the Rye*, (New York: Bay Back Books, 2001), 205, first published 1951.

[71] Nancie George, "10 Incredible Facts About Your Sense of Smell," *Everyday Health*, last modified October 3, 2014, accessed July 2017, http://www.everydayhealth.com/news/incredible-facts-about-your-sense-smell/.

[72] "Thinking Sensing and Behaving," Brain Facts, accessed July 2017, http://www.brainfacts.org/sensing-thinking-behaving/senses-and-perception/articles/2015/making-sense-of-scents-smell-and-the-brain/.

[73] Leonard Sax, M.D., "Why Stinky Socks May Bother Women More Than Men," *The New York Times*, August 30, 2017, https://www.nytimes.com/2017/08/30/well/family/why-stinky-socks-may-bother-women-more-than-men.html.

[74] Wikipedia, s.v. "Hyposmia," last modified December 3, 2015, 17:37, https://en.wikipedia.org/wiki/Hyposmia.

[75] Wikipedia, s.v. "Anosmia," last modified February 18, 2018, 11:47, https://en.wikipedia.org/wiki/Anosmia.

[76] "Smell Disorders," National Institute on Deafness and Other Communication Disorders, last modified May 12, 2017, https://www.nidcd.nih.gov/health/smell-disorders.

[77] "Sleep Apnea," National Heart, Lung and Blood Institute, accessed August 2017, https://www.nhlbi.nih.gov/health/health-topics/topics/sleepapnea/.

[78] "Nasal Obstruction," Fort Worth ENT, accessed August 2017, http://fortworthent.net/ear-nose-throat/snoring-obstructive-sleep-apnea-osa/nasal-obstruction/.

[79] "Deviated Septum," WebMD, accessed August 2017, http://www.webmd.com/allergies/deviated-septum#1.

[80] Kay Halle, *Irrepressible Churchill: A Treasury of Winston Churchill's Wit*, (New York and Cleveland: World Publishing Company, 1966), 263.

[81] "How does our sense of taste work?" PubMed Health, last modified August 17, 2016, https://www.ncbi.nlm.nih.gov/pubmedhealth/PMH0072592/.

[82] "Taste Disorders," MedicineNet, accessed August 2017, http://www.medicinenet.com/taste_disorders/article.htm.

[83] In Hervey Allen's *Anthony Adverse*, 1933, as quoted in:
  Robert Andrews, *The Columbia Dictionary of Quotations*, (New York: Columbia University Press, 1993), 585.

[84] Laura Moss, "What is synesthesia and what's it like to have it?" *Mother Nature Network*, October 5, 2014, accessed August 2017, www.mnn.com/health/fitness-well-being/stories/what-is-synesthesia-and-whats-it-like-to-have-it.

[85] M. Synesthi and Nic Swaner, "10 Disadvantages to Synesthesia," *ListVerse*, September 2, 2012, https://listverse.com/2012/09/02/10-disadvantages-to-synesthesia/.

[86] "What is Insomnia?" National Sleep Foundation, accessed August 2017, https://sleepfoundation.org/insomnia/content/what-is-insomnia.

[87] Paula Alhola and Päivi Polo-Kantola, "Sleep deprivation: Impact on cognitive performance," *National Center for Biotechnology Information*, accessed August 2017, https://www.ncbi.nlm.nih.gov/pmc/articles/PMC2656292/.

[88] "What is autism?" The National Autistic Society, accessed August 2017, http://www.autism.org.uk/about/what-is.aspx.

[89] "Autism Spectrum Disorder," Centers for Disease Control and Prevention, accessed August 2017, http://www.cdc.gov/ncbddd/autism/data.html.

[90] "Sensory differences," The National Autistic Society, accessed August 2017, http://www.autism.org.uk/sensory.

[91] René Descartes, Discourse on *Method of Rightly Conducting One's Reason and of Seeking the Truth in the Sciences*, (1637), Part IV.

[92] Oxford Reference, s.v. "Opportunity Cost," accessed September 2017, http://www.oxfordreference.com/view/10.1093/oi/authority.20110810105528518.

[93] J. M. Barrie, *The Plays of J. M. Barrie: The Admirable Crichton*, (New York: Charles Scribner's Sons, 1922), 12.

[94] "Mortality and global health estimates country statistical profiles," World Health Organization, accessed September 2017, http://www.who.int/gho/mortality_burden_disease/countries/en/.

[95] Pearl Jam, *Do the Evolution*, (Los Angeles: Epic Records, 1998).

[96] Lita Cosner, "How does the Bible teach 6,000 years?" Creation, accessed September 2017, https://creation.com/6000-years.

[97] Nola Taylor Redd, "How Old is Earth?" Space, February 27, 2014, https://www.space.com/24854-how-old-is-earth.html.

[98] "Napoleon on War," Napoleonic Guide, accessed March 2017, http://www.napoleonguide.com/maxim_war.htm.

[99] Wikipedia, s.v. "Flag Desecration Amendment," last modified February 16, 2018, 02:43, wikipedia.org/wiki/Flag_Desecration_Amendment.

[100] The Official Website for The State of New Jersey, accessed September 2017, http://nj.gov/governor/news/news/552017/approved/20170614a.html.

[101] Virginia Woolf quote accessed from:
Sarah McKeown, "Language is wine upon the lips," Macmillan Dictionary Blog, accessed March 2017, http://www.macmillandictionaryblog.com/language-is-wine-upon-the-lips.

[102] O. Henry, *The Complete Works of O. Henry*, (New York: Garden City Publishing Company, Inc., 1911), 152.

[103] "Income Inequality," Inequality, accessed September 2017, https://inequality.org/facts/income-inequality/.

[104] Jim Valvano, *Arthur Ashe Courage Award Acceptance* Address, March 1993, https://www.youtube.com/watch?v=SHKzH6zR8xE.

[105] J. K. Rowling, *Harry Potter and the Goblet of Fire*, (London: Bloomsbury, 2000).

[106] "Mario Andredtti Quotable Quote," Goodreads, accessed April 2017, https://www.goodreads.com/quotes/13356-if-everything-seems-under-control-you-re-not-going-fast-enough.

[107] Quotation by Ernest Hemingway:
Pass It On, accessed September 2017, https://www.passiton.com/inspirational-quotes/7520-courage-is-grace-under-pressure.

[108] "Ray Kroc," Biography, last modified August 29, 2017, accessed September 2017, https://www.biography.com/people/ray-kroc-9369349.

[109] "New Jersey Minimum Wage," InsideGov, accessed September 2017, http://minimum-wage.insidegov.com/l/31/New-Jersey.

[110] McDonald's Wiki, s.v. "Grimace," accessed September 2017, http://mcdonalds.wikia.com/wiki/Grimace.

[111] Quote Attributed to poet Robert Burns (1759-1796) but unverified:
Wikipedia, s.v. "Robert Burns," last modified January 3, 2018, 13:35, https://en.wikiquote.org/wiki/Robert_Burns.

[112] "Ponzi Scheme," Investopedia, accessed September 2017, www.investopedia.com/terms/p/ponzischeme.asp.

[113] Wikipedia, s.v. "Madoff investment scandal," last modified February 21, 2018, 00:03, wikipedia.org/wiki/Madoff_investment_scandal.

[114] "Sampling Bias," in *Encyclopedia of Survey Research Methods*, edited by Paul J. Lavrakas, 2008, methods.sagepub.com/reference/encyclopedia-of-survey-research-methods/n509.xml.

[115] "John Maynard Keynes Quotable Quote," Goodreads, accessed September 2017, https://www.goodreads.com/quotes/552847-when-the-capital-development-of-a-country-becomes-a-by-product.

116 "Size of the online gambling market from 2009 to 2020 (in billion U.S. dollars)," Statista, accessed September 2017, https://www.statista.com/statistics/270728/market-volume-of-online-gaming-worldwide/.

117 "Shuffle Master," SS Gaming, accessed September 2017, www.sggaming.com/Shuffle-Master.

118 "Monkeys are Better Stockpickers Than You'd Think," Barrons, accessed September 2017, www.barrons.com/articles/monkeys-are-better-stockpickers-than-youd-think-1403206862.

119 From the film *Contact* based on the book by Carl Sagan:
    Contact, directed by Robert Zemeckis, written by James V. Hart and Michael Goldenberg, (Burbank: Warner Brothers, 1997).

120 This quote has been attributed to playwright Diane Grant, but it is unconfirmed:
    AZ Quotes, accessed September 2017, http://www.azquotes.com/quote/536852.

121 *Merriam-Webster*, s.v. "groupthink (n.)," accessed October 2017, https://www.merriam-webster.com/dictionary/groupthink.

122 Wikipedia, s.v. "Flat Earth," last modified February 26, 2018, 05:25, https://en.wikipedia.org/wiki/Flat_Earth.

123 Helen Armitage, "10 Inventions No One Thought Would Be a Success," *The Culture Trip*, August 11, 2017, accessed October 2017, https://theculturetrip.com/north-america/usa/articles/10-inventions-no-one-thought-would-be-a-success/.

124 Ibid

125 Yahoo Finance, accessed October 2017, https://finance.yahoo.com/quote/amzn?p=amzn.

126 William Blake, *The Marriage of Heaven and Hell*, accessed on Bartleby, originally published 1790, lines 115-116, http://www.bartleby.com/235/253.html.

127 "Ralph Waldo Emerson," Goodreads, accessed September 2017, https://www.goodreads.com/author/show/12080.Ralph_Waldo_Emerson.

128 "The most spoken languages worldwide (native speakers in millions)," Statista, accessed November 2017, https://www.statista.com/statistics/266808/the-most-spoken-languages-worldwide/.

129 "Prevalence of tinnitus," Hear-it, accessed November 2017, https://www.hear-it.org/prevalence-tinnitus.

130 Christine Negroni, "How Much of the World's Population Has Flown in an Airplane?" *Air & Space Smithsonian Magazine*, January 6, 2016, https://www.airspacemag.com/daily-planet/how-much-worlds-population-has-flown-airplane-180957719/.

131 "What is 20/20 Vision?" *University of Iowa Hospitals and Clinics*, accessed November 2017, https://uihc.org/health-library/what-2020-vision.

132 Katie Kens, "11 Little-Known Facts About Left-Handers," Huffpost, October 29, 2012, https://www.huffingtonpost.com/2012/10/29/left-handed-facts-lefties_n_2005864.html.

[133] Original French quote by:

> Pierre-Marc-Gaston de Levis, *Maximes et réflexions sur differents sujets de morale et de politique*, Volume 1, 4th ed. (Paris: Renouard, 1812).
> Translation from:
> Wikiquote, s.v. "Voltaire," last modified February 25, 2018, 23:08, https://en.wiki-quote.org/wiki/Voltaire.

[134] "Confucius Quotable Quote," Goodreads, accessed April 2017, https://www.goodreads.com/quotes/63436-attack-the-evil-that-is-within-yourself-rather-than-attacking.

[135] "Billie Jean King Quotable Quote," Goodreads, accessed April 2017, https://www.goodreads.com/quotes/209337-champions-keep-playing-until-they-get-it-right.

[136] U.S. Declaration of Independence, July 4, 1776, accessed on National Archives, https://www.archives.gov/founding-docs/declaration-transcript.

BIBLIOGRAPHY:

Access to Insight. "What is Theravada Buddhism?" Accessed
    February 2017. https://www.accesstoinsight.org/theravada.html.

Alessandra, Tony. "The Platinum Rule." Accessed March 2017.
    http://www.alessandra.com/abouttony/aboutpr.asp

Alhola, Paula and Päivi Polo-Kantola. "Sleep deprivation: Impact on
    cognitive performance." *National Center for Biotechnology Information*. Accessed August
    2017. https://www.ncbi.nlm.nih.gov/pmc/articles/PMC2656292/.

American Academy of Dermatology. "Psoriasis." Accessed July 2017.
    www.aad.org/media/stats/conditions/psoriasis.

American Psychological Association. "*Stress in America: The State
    of Our Nation.*" Published November 1, 2017. https://www.apa.org/news/press/releases/
    stress/2017/state-nation.pdf.

Anderson, Stephen R. "How many languages are there in the
    world?" *Linguistic Society of America*. Accessed April 2017. https://www.linguisticsociety.
    org/content/how-many-languages-are-there-world.

Andrews, Robert. *The Columbia Dictionary of Quotations*. New York:
    Columbia University Press, 1993.

Armitage, Helen. "10 Inventions No One Thought Would Be a
    Success." *The Culture Trip*. August 11, 2017. Accessed October 2017. https://theculture-
    trip.com/north-america/usa/articles/10-inventions-no-one-thought-would-be-a-success/.

AZ Quotes. Accessed September 2017.
    http://www.azquotes.com/quote/536852.

Bacon, Francis. *The Advancement of Learning*. Originally published
    1605. New York: Project Gutenburg, 2014. https://www.gutenberg.org/files/5500/5500-
    h/5500-h.htm.

Barrie, J. M., *The Plays of J. M. Barrie: The Admirable Crichton*. New
    York: Charles Scribner's Sons, 1922.

Barrons. "Monkeys are Better Stockpickers Than You'd Think."
    Accessed September 2017. www.barrons.com/articles/monkeys-are-better-stockpickers-
    than-youd-think-1403206862.

Biography. "Plato." Accessed March 2018.
    https://www.biography.com/people/plato-9442588.

Biography. "Ray Kroc." Last modified August 29, 2017. Accessed
    September 2017. https://www.biography.com/people/ray-kroc-9369349.

Blake, William. *The Marriage of Heaven and Hell*. Accessed on
    Bartleby. Originally published 1790. http://www.bartleby.com/235/253.html.

133

Brain Facts. "Thinking Sensing and Behaving." Accessed July 2017.
http://www.brainfacts.org/sensing-thinking-behaving/senses-and-perception/arti-
cles/2015/making-sense-of-scents-smell-and-the-brain/.

Centers for Disease Control and Prevention. "Autism Spectrum
Disorder." Accessed August 2017. http://www.cdc.gov/ncbddd/autism/data.html.

Colourblindor. "Ishihara's Test for Colour Deficiency: 38 Plates
Edition." Accessed May 2017. http://www.color-blindness.com/ishiharas-test-for-co-
lour-deficiency-38-plates-edition/.

Contact. Directed by Robert Zemeckis, written by James V. Hart and
Michael Goldenberg. Burbank: Warner Brothers, 1997.

Cosner, Lita. "How does the Bible teach 6,000 years?" *Creation.*
Accessed September 2017. https://creation.com/6000-years.

De Levis, Pierre-Marc-Gaston. *Maximes et réflexions sur différents
sujets de morale et de politique.* Volume 1, 4th ed. Paris: Renouard, 1812.

Descartes, René. *Discourse on Method of Rightly Conducting One's
Reason and of Seeking the Truth in the Sciences.* 1637.

Emerson, Ralph Waldo. "Experience" in *Essays: Second Series.*
Boston: James Munroe.
1844. Found on American Transcendentalism Web.
http://transcendentalism-legacy.tamu.edu/authors/emerson/essays/experience.html.

Encyclopedia of Survey Research Methods. "Sampling Bias."
Edited by Paul J. Lavrakas. 2008. methods.sagepub.com/reference/encyclopedia-of-sur-
vey-research-methods/n509.xml.

Exodus 20:2-17. *The Bible*: The Old Testament. Bible Info. Accessed
March 2017. http://www.bibleinfo.com/en/topics/ten-commandments.

Eye Health Web. "Astigmatism." Accessed May 2017.
http://www.eyehealthweb.com/astigmatism/.

Fort Lauderdale Eye Institute. "Difference Between Near and Far
Sighted." Accessed July 2017. www.flei.com/blog/difference-between-near-and-farsight-
ed/.

Fort Worth ENT. "Nasal Obstruction." Accessed August 2017.
http://fortworthent.net/ear-nose-throat/snoring-obstructive-sleep-apnea-osa/nasal-ob-
struction/.

Frost, Robert. *Mountain Interval.*
New York: Henry Holt and Company, 1916.

Genesis 11:9. *The Bible.* Accessed April, 2017.
http://biblehub.com/genesis.

George, Nancie. "10 Incredible Facts About Your Sense of Smell."
Everyday Health. Last modified October 3, 2014. Accessed July 2017. http://www.every-
dayhealth.com/news/incredible-facts-about-your-sense-smell/.

Goodreads. "Billie Jean King Quotable Quote." Accessed April
        2017. https://www.goodreads.com/quotes/209337-champions-keep-playing-until-they-
        get-it-right.

Goodreads. "Confucius Quotable Quote." Accessed April 2017.
        https://www.goodreads.com/quotes/63436-attack-the-evil-that-is-within-yourself-rather-
        than-attacking.

Goodreads. "George Carlin Quotable Quotes." Accessed March
        2017. https://www.goodreads.com/quotes/7926-meow-means-woof-in-cat.

Goodreads. "Gustave Flaubert Quotable Quote." Accessed July
        2017. https://www.goodreads.com/quotes/46318-never-touch-your-idols-the-gilding-
        will-stick-to-your.

Goodreads. "John Maynard Keynes Quotable Quote." Accessed
        September 2017. https://www.goodreads.com/quotes/552847-when-the-capital-develop-
        ment-of-a-country-becomes-a-by-product.

Goodreads. "Mario Andredtti Quotable Quote." Accessed April
        2017. https://www.goodreads.com/quotes/13356-if-everything-seems-under-control-
        you-re-not-going-fast-enough.

Goodreads. "Ralph Waldo Emerson." Accessed September 2017.
        https://www.goodreads.com/author/show/12080.Ralph_Waldo_Emerson.

Google Translate. Accessed March 2017.

Greene, Brian. *The Fabric of the Cosmos: Space, Time and The
        Texture of Reality*. New York: Vintage Books, 2005.

Gregoire, Carolyn. "How Our Sense of Touch Affects Everything We
        Do." *Huffington Post*. January 20, 2015. Accessed July 2017. http://www.huffingtonpost.
        com/2015/01/20/neuroscience-touch_n_6489050.html.

Halle, Kay. *Irrepressible Churchill: A Treasury of Winston Churchill's
        Wit*. New York and Cleveland: World Publishing Company, 1966.

Healthline. "Astigmatism." Accessed May 2017.
        http://www.healthline.com/health/astigmatism#overview1.

Hear It. "Your ears differ." Accessed June 2017.
        http://www.hear-it.org/Your-ears-differ-.

Hear-it. "Prevalence of tinnitus." Accessed November 2017.
        https://www.hear-it.org/prevalence-tinnitus.

Henry, O. *The Complete Works of O. Henry*. New York: Garden City
        Publishing Company, Inc., 1911.

Hoffman, Howard J., MA; Robert A. Dobie, MD; Katalin G. Losonczy,
        MA, et al. "Declining Prevalence of Hearing Loss in Us Adults Aged 20 to 69 Years."
        JAMA. March 2017. https://jamanetwork.com/journals/jamaotolaryngology/article-ab-
        stract/2592954.

Inequality. "Income Inequality." Accessed September 2017,
https://inequality.org/facts/income-inequality/.

InsideGov. "New Jersey Minimum Wage." Accessed September
2017. http://minimum-wage.insidegov.com/l/31/New-Jersey.

Investopedia. "Ponzi Scheme." Accessed September 2017.
www.investopedia.com/terms/p/ponzischeme.asp.

Jung, C. G. *Visions: notes of the seminar given in 1930-1934*. Edited
by Claire Douglas. Princeton: Princeton University Press, 1997.

Keats, John. "Ode on a Grecian Urn." 1820.

Kens, Katie. "11 Little-Known Facts About Left-Handers."
Huffpost. October 29, 2012. https://www.huffingtonpost.com/2012/10/29/left-handed-facts-lefties_n_2005864.html.

Knowledge Nuts. "Why Everyone Hears the Same Sounds
Differently." March 31, 2016. Accessed June 2017. http://knowledgenuts.com/2016/03/31/why-everyone-hears-the-same-sounds-differently/.

Living With Faith. "The Generous Eye." Accessed March 2017.
http://www.livingwithfaith.org/blog/the-generous-eye.

Locke, John. *An Essay Concerning Humane Understanding*.
London: 1689. http://www.earlymoderntexts.com/assets/pdfs/locke1690book1.pdf.

Locke, John. *Second Treatise of Government*. 1690; Project
Gutenberg, 2010. https://www.gutenberg.org/files/7370/7370-h/7370-h.htm.

Math Planet. "The Pythagorean Theorem." Accessed January
2017. https://www.mathplanet.com/education/pre-algebra/right-triangles-and-algebra/the-pythagorean-theorem.

McDonald's Wiki. S.v. "Grimace." Accessed September 2017.
http://mcdonalds.wikia.com/wiki/Grimace.

McKeown, Sarah. "Language is wine upon the lips." Macmillan
Dictionary Blog. Accessed March 2017. http://www.macmillandictionaryblog.com/language-is-wine-upon-the-lips.

McPherson, James. "A Defining Time in Our Nation's History." Civil
War Trust. Accessed March 2017. https://www.civilwar.org/learn/articles/brief-overview-american-civil-war.

MedicineNet. "Taste Disorders." Accessed August 2017.
http://www.medicinenet.com/taste_disorders/article.htm.

Medline Plus. "Aging changes in the senses." Accessed June 2017.
https://medlineplus.gov/ency/article/004013.htm.

Merriam-Webster. S.v. "groupthink (n.)." Accessed October
2017. https://www.merriam-webster.com/dictionary/groupthink.

Merriam-Webster, S.v. "law (n.)." Accessed December 2016.
https://www.merriam-webster.com/dictionary/law.

Merriam-Webster. S.v. "relativity (n.)." Accessed December 2016.
https://www.merriam-webster.com/dictionary/relativity.

Merriam-Webster. S.v. "ubiquity (n.)." Accessed December 2016.
https://www.merriam-webster.com/dictionary/ubiquity.

Merriam-Webster. S.v., "universal (adj.)." Accessed December
2016. https://www.merriam-webster.com/dictionary/universal.

Milanovich, Norma and Shirley D. McCune. *The Light Shall Set You Free*. Kalispell: Athena Publishing, 1996.

More, Thomas. Utopia. 1516.

Moss, Laura. "What is synesthesia and what's it like to have it?"
Mother Nature Network. October 5, 2014. Accessed August 2017. www.mnn.com/health/fitness-well-being/stories/what-is-synesthesia-and-whats-it-like-to-have-it.

Napoleonic Guide. "Napoleon on War." Accessed March 2017.
http://www.napoleonguide.com/maxim_war.htm.

National Eye Institute. "Facts About Color Blindness." Accessed May
2017. https://nei.nih.gov/health/color_blindness/facts_about.

National Eye Institute. "Farsightedness." Accessed May 2017.
https://www.nei.nih.gov/sites/default/files/health-pdfs/Farsightedness.

National Heart, Lung and Blood Institute. "Sleep Apnea." Accessed
August 2017. https://www.nhlbi.nih.gov/health/health-topics/topics/sleepapnea/.

National Institute on Deafness and Other Communication Disorders.
"Quick Statistics About Hearing." Accessed June 2017. https://www.nidcd.nih.gov/health/statistics/quick-statistics-hearing.

National Institute on Deafness and Other Communication Disorders.
"Smell Disorders." Last modified May 12, 2017. https://www.nidcd.nih.gov/health/smell-disorders.

National Sleep Foundation. "What is Insomnia?" Accessed August
2017. https://sleepfoundation.org/insomnia/content/what-is-insomnia.

Negroni, Christine. "How Much of the World's Population Has
Flown in an Airplane?" *Air & Space Smithsonian Magazine*. January 6, 2016. https://www.airspacemag.com/daily-planet/how-much-worlds-population-has-flown-air-plane-180957719/.

Ossola, Alexandra. "The World is Rapidly Becoming More
Nearsighted." Popular Science. February 18, 2016. http://www.popsci.com/nearly-5-bil-lion-people-will-be-nearsighted-by-2050.

Oxford Reference. S.v. "Opportunity Cost." Accessed September 2017.
http://www.oxfordreference.com/view/10.1093/oi/authority.20110810105528518.

Pass It On. Accessed September 2017.
https://www.passiton.com/inspirational-quotes/7520-courage-is-grace-under-pressure.

Patient. "Hearing Tests." Accessed May 2017. https://patient.info/doctor/hearing-tests-pro.

Pearl Jam. *Do the Evolution*. Los Angeles: Epic Records, 1998.

Philosophy Index. "Meta-Ethics." Accessed March 2017.
http://www.philosophy-index.com/ethics/meta-ethics/.

PubMed Health. "How does our sense of taste work?" Last modified
August 17, 2016. https://www.ncbi.nlm.nih.gov/pubmedhealth/PMH0072592/.

Quote Investigator. "It Has Become Appallingly Obvious That Our
Technology Has Exceeded Our Humanity." Accessed March 2017. https://quoteinvestigator.com/2012/10/25/tech-exceeded/.

Rand, Ayn. *Atlas Shrugged*. New York: Random House, 1957.

Rand, Robert W. "How many people have vestibular disorders?"
Rand Acoustics. Accessed June 2017. http://randacoustics.com/how-many-people-have-vestibular-disorders/.

Redd, Nola Taylor. "How Old is Earth?" *Space*. February 27, 2014.
https://www.space.com/24854-how-old-is-earth.html.

Religion Facts. "Five Pillars of Islam." Accessed February 2017.
http://www.religionfacts.com/five-pillars-islam.

Rothstein, Dave. "Do we see the same stars from above and below
the equator?" Cornell Education. Last modified December 10, 2015. http://curious.astro.cornell.edu/about-us/120-observational-astronomy/stargazing/how-the-motion-of-the-earth-affects-our-view/732-do-we-see-the-same-stars-from-above-and-below-the-equator-beginner.

Rowling, J. K. *Harry Potter and the Goblet of Fire*. London:
Bloomsbury, 2000.

Salinger, J.D. *The Catcher in the Rye*. New York: Bay Back Books,
2001. First published 1951.

Sax, Leonard M.D. "Why Stinky Socks May Bother Women More
Than Men." *The New York Times*. August 30, 2017. https://www.nytimes.com/2017/08/30/well/family/why-stinky-socks-may-bother-women-more-than-men.html.

Shakespeare, William. *Hamlet*. Edited by Barbara A. Mowat and
Paul Werstine. New York: Simon & Schuster, 2012.

SS Gaming. "Shuffle Master." Accessed September 2017.
www.sggaming.com/Shuffle-Master.

Statista. "Size of the online gambling market from 2009 to 2020 (in
billion U.S. dollars)." Accessed September 2017. https://www.statista.com/statistics/270728/market-volume-of-online-gaming-worldwide/.

Statista. "The most spoken languages worldwide (native
speakers in millions)." Accessed November 2017. https://www.statista.com/statis-
tics/266808/the-most-spoken-languages-worldwide/.

Synesthi, M. and Nic Swaner. "10 Disadvantages to Synesthesia."
ListVerse. September 2, 2012. https://listverse.com/2012/09/02/10-disadvantages-to-syn-
esthesia/.

The Bible. King James Version.

The Bible. New International Version.

The National Autistic Society. "Sensory differences." Accessed
August 2017. http://www.autism.org.uk/sensory.

The National Autistic Society. "What is autism?" Accessed August
2017. http://www.autism.org.uk/about/what-is.aspx.

The Official Website for The State of New Jersey. Accessed
September 2017. http://nj.gov/governor/news/news/552017/approved/20170614a.html.

Thornstein, Hazel. "Names of Tactile Disorders." *Livestrong*. June
13, 2017. Accessed July 2017. http://www.livestrong.com/article/172305-names-of-tac-
tile-disorders/.

U.S. Declaration of Independence. July 4, 1776. Accessed on
National Archives. https://www.archives.gov/founding-docs/declaration-transcript.

U.S. Department of Health and Human Services Centers for Disease
Control and Prevention, National Center for Health Statistics. "Summary health
statistics for U.S. adults: National Health Interview Survey," 2012. Hyattsville: DHHS
Publication, February 2014. https://www.cdc.gov/nchs/data/series/sr_10/sr10_260.pdf.

United Nations. "Universal Declaration of Human Rights."
December 10, 1948. http://www.un.org/en/universal-declaration-human-rights/.

University of Iowa Hospitals & Clinics. "What is 20/20 Vision?"
Accessed May 2017. https://uihc.org/health-library/what-2020-vision.

Valvano, Jim. *Arthur Ashe Courage Award Acceptance Address*.
March 1993. https://www.youtube.com/watch?v=SHKzH6zR8xE.

WebMD. "Deviated Septum." Accessed August 2017.
http://www.webmd.com/allergies/deviated-septum#1.

WebMD. "Understanding Psoriasis—the Basics." Accessed July
2017. https://www.webmd.com/skin-problems-and-treatments/psoriasis/understand-
ing-psoriasis-basics#1.

WebMD. "Understanding Tinnitus Basics." Accessed June 2017.
http://www.webmd.com/a-to-z-guides/understanding-tinnitus-basics.

WebMD. "Vertigo." Accessed June 2017.
http://www.webmd.com/brain/vertigo-symptoms-causes-treatment#1.

Whorf, Benjamin. Language, Thought and Reality. Cambridge: Technology Press of Massachusetts Institute of Technology, 1956.

Wikipedia. S.v. "Ancient Greece." Last modified February 13, 2018. 18:51. https://en.wikipedia.org/wiki/Ancient_Greece.

Wikipedia. S.v. "Anosmia." Last modified February 18, 2018, 11:47. https://en.wikipedia.org/wiki/Anosmia.

Wikipedia. S.v. "Flag Desecration Amendment." Last modified February 16, 2018, 02:43. wikipedia.org/wiki/Flag_Desecration_Amendment.

Wikipedia. S.v. "Flat Earth." Last modified February 26, 2018, 05:25. https://en.wikipedia.org/wiki/Flat_Earth.

Wikipedia. S.v. "Groundwork of the Metaphysics of Morals." Last modified December 4, 2017, 13:53. https://en.wikipedia.org/wiki/Groundwork_of_the_Metaphysic_of_Morals.

Wikipedia. S.v. "Hyposmia." Last modified December 3, 2015, 17:37. https://en.wikipedia.org/wiki/Hyposmia.

Wikipedia. S.v. "If a tree falls in a forest (George Berkeley)." Last modified February 1, 2018, 03:17. https://en.wikipedia.org/wiki/If_a_tree_falls_in_a_forest.

Wikipedia. S.v. "Madoff investment scandal." Last modified February 21, 2018, 00:03. wikipedia.org/wiki/Madoff_investment_scandal.

Wikipedia. S.v. "Robert Burns." Last modified January 3, 2018, 13:35. https://en.wikiquote.org/wiki/Robert_Burns.

Wikiquote. S.v. "Voltaire." Last modified February 25, 2018, 23:08. https://en.wikiquote.org/wiki/Voltaire.

World Emoji Day. Accessed March 2017. http://worldemojiday.com.

World Health Organization. "Global Health Observatory (GHO) data." Accessed March, 2017. http://www.who.int/gho/mortality_burden_disease/life_tables/situation_trends/en/.

World Health Organization. "Mortality and global health estimates country statistical profiles." Accessed September 2017. http://www.who.int/gho/mortality_burden_disease/countries/en/.

Worldometers. Accessed December 2016. http://www.worldometers.info.

Yahoo Finance. Accessed October 2017. https://finance.yahoo.com/quote/amzn?p=amzn.

Zimmerman, Kim Ann. "Declarative Memory: Definitions & Examples." Live Science. February 5, 2014. Accessed March 2017. https://www.livescience.com/43153-declarative-memory.html.

ABOUT THE AUTHOR:

Ian Winer

I an Winer connects people to the truth of market places and human behavior. His unique approach to analyzing and predicting outcomes is built on his philosophy of "Ubiquitous Relativity," a phrase he coined in 2016 after a chance encounter picking his nose at a stop light. In the world of finance, his trademark offering is a source of fun and entertaining insight into markets that, more often than not, are born from his uniquely non-consensus thinking.

At the heart of Winer's Ubiquitous Relativity philosophy, which he credits for his success, is the ability to "push pause on judgment" and focus on the fun of the human experience in every piece of analysis. He was so moved by this philosophy that he decided to leave a career in finance after 22 years to pursue it in greater detail. In other words, he decided it was time to "walk the walk."

A West Point graduate, Winer was the first United States Military Academy graduate to play in the Division 1 Ice Hockey All-Star game. A survivor of abuse, addiction, and "fear based" living, Winer spent his early years searching for the "answer" to life's major question of "Can I make a difference in this life?" An epiphany in the form of "Ubiquitous Relativity" changed his entire perception of the world. Living through multiple boom and bust cycles and personally going from penthouse to outhouse, Winer's story is one of rising from the ashes where we can all take heed.

Ian Winer and his wife Kelly have committed to a year of volunteering around the world and trying to make a difference in the lives of others.

Ian@IanWiner.com

IanWiner.com

Instagram.com/IanWinerMyTruth

TVGUESTPERT PUBLISHING

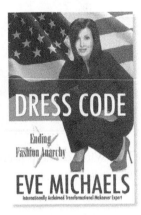

JACK H. HARRIS
Father of the Blob: The Making of a Monster Smash and Other Hollywood Tales
Paperback: $16.95
Kindle/Nook: $9.99

New York Times Best Seller
CHRISTY WHITMAN
The Art of Having It All: A Woman's Guide to Unlimited Abundance
Paperback: $16.95
Kindle/Nook: $9.99
Audible Book: $13.00

EVE MICHAELS
Dress Code: Ending Fashion Anarchy
Paperback: $15.95
Kindle/Nook: $9.99
Audible Book: $17.95

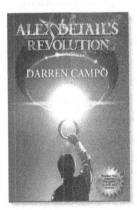

DARREN CAMPO
Alex Detail's Revolution
Paperback: $9.95
Hardcover: $22.95
Kindle: $9.15

DARREN CAMPO
Alex Detail's Rebellion
Hardcover: $22.95
Kindle: $9.99

DARREN CAMPO
Disappearing Spell: Generationist Files: Book 1
Kindle: $2.99

TVGuestpert Publishing
11664 National Blvd, #345
Los Angeles, CA. 90064
310-584-1504
www.TVGPublishing.com

GAYANI DESILVA, MD
A Psychiatrist's Guide: Stop Teen Addiction Before It Starts
Paperback: $16.95
Kindle: $9.99

GAYANI DeSILVA, MD
A Psychiatrist's Guide: Helping Parents Reach Their Depressed Tween
Paperback: $16.95
Kindle: $9.99

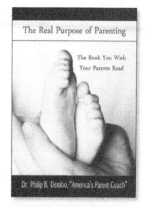

DR. PHILIP DEMBO
The Real Purpose of Parenting: The Book You Wish Your Parents Read
Paperback: $15.95
Kindle: $9.99
Audible: $23.95

JACQUIE JORDAN AND SHANNON O'DOWD
The Ultimate On-Camera Guidebook: Hosts*Experts*Influencers
Paperback: $16.95
Kindle: $9.99

JACQUIE JORDAN
Heartfelt Marketing: Allowing the Universe to be Your Business Partner
Paperback: $15.95
Kindle: $9.99
Audible: $9.95

JACQUIE JORDAN
Get on TV! The Insider's Guide to Pitching the Producers and Promoting Yourself
Published by Sourcebooks
Paperback: $14.95
Kindle: $9.99
Nook: $14.95